What's Happening to Catholic Schools?

the flickering light

by
Frances Forde Plude

William H. Sadlier, Inc.
New York ● Chicago ● Los Angeles

ISBN 0-8215-6500-1
123456789/987654

For Donald and Thomas—
each "a man for all seasons"

CONTENTS

ACKNOWLEDGMENTS

The interesting thing about learning is one rarely does it alone; one is constantly in dialogue—with writers, with colleagues, with family and with friends.

My own educational growth has been such a dialogue and I should publicly acknowledge my indebtedness to some who have had the patience to teach me.

Oldest among them was a ninety-year old woman who died before this book was finished, but whose interest in education helped inspire it. My grandmother was a schoolteacher from another era, but she always cherished the educational bond between herself, my mother, and me—three generations of schoolteachers.

Boston College provided my basis for dialogue, and over ten years in Catholic education provided many opportunities. Prominent as my models over this decade have been Monsignor Timothy F. O'Leary, Brother Raymund F. Davey, Monsignor Walter L. Flaherty, and Dr. James T. McDonough, Jr. Each one has guided my search in unique ways.

Because an open teacher learns from students, I hope my generation gap dissolves when I dialogue with young people.

Probably my greatest debt is to the individual who has been my teacher in more than a dozen years of marriage. This book is a tribute to his patience and understanding.

Frances Forde Plude

7

INTRODUCTION

Remember how easy it was to be a Catholic ten or twenty years ago? Many Catholic parents must long for "the good old days" when it was so simple. You listened to what the priest said, never questioned his authority, and you passed all this along to your children, to the best of your ability and theirs.

Where did it all go?

Today newspaper headlines and magazine articles are startling. Here's a sample:

"Has the Church Lost Its Soul?"[1]

"Can the Catholic Revolution Succeed?"[2]

"The Catholic Crisis"[3]

It certainly is too simple to explain all these changes with the two words *Vatican Council*. And yet, in 1959, when Pope John XXIII called for an Ecumenical Council, we were driven into a new era in the Church. In the process of shifting gears to enter this new age, we have had some accidents and even a significant number of casualties.

Many articles and books have been written to analyze changes within the Roman Catholic Church. Much of this material has been outstanding. Some men and women — within religious orders and outside of them — have earned much respect for their intelligent and polished explanation of "what's going on" in the Catholic Church today, and what to expect in years to come.

Then, of course, there is the other kind.

Some of the material written has been of the "scandal sheet" variety. These writers try to shock rather than enlighten their readers.

The great majority of Americans have not been helped much by either type of writing.

The scholarly analysis is valuable to professional educators and Church leaders. But parents can get headaches wading through statistical tables and the jargon professionals use when speaking to one another. The theologian's careful analysis of problems, and the university professor's research are both vital to the thinking process of any Church. Those who subscribe to magazines such as *Theological Studies, America,* or *The Catholic World* can participate in this thinking process with the professionals as they summarize their theories.

However, the total number of subscribers to all three of these magazines is only about 85,000.[4] The total Catholic population in America is over 48 million.[5] Many of these millions, especially the parents among that number, want to know what is happening to the Catholic schools they have built and financed. Are parents to be given nothing but a choice between statistical tables and scandal sheets?

That is why this book came into existence.

The Flickering Light has been written for people who have neither the time nor the inclination to read the rather deep material written by the professional thinkers in the Roman Catholic Church. It is an honest attempt to explain what is happening within American Catholic education. I have tried to create a book that would be thought-provoking, accurate, and helpful, without being stuffy, and without being scandalous.

These ideas and observations are presented by a person who has worked within Catholic education as a professional for over ten years. Much of this time has been spent absorbing and analyzing the material flowing from the pens of theologians and sociologists. This combination of professional experience and study provides the basis for this book.

The chief aim of the book, however, is to present a sane analysis which any American can read and enjoy. Hopefully, such a calm appraisal would benefit all taxpayers—Catholic and non-Catholic alike.

Frances Forde Plude

PROLOGUE

The Flickering Light analyzes vigorous attempts now underway in the Catholic Church to renew, broaden, and redesign the Church's educational systems.

Catholic education seems to be emerging vitally renewed from ominous shadows. Recent legal setbacks, such as the Supreme Court decision of 1973, have struck down aid to parents of non-public school students. Yet these reverses have failed to discourage Catholic support of a separate school system. In fact, reports from all over the country indicate increased support for Catholic education. Undaunted, Catholic leaders—and, most importantly, Catholic parents—seem more determined than ever to preserve and foster the Catholic school system. Fully aware of the financial problems involved, Catholic parents are expressing a gratifying dedication to the ideals of Catholic education and an appreciation of the value of educational choice.

Catholic schools are different where it counts—in message, community, and service. They are, as the bishops of the United States affirmed in their 1972 educational pastoral, "the best expression of the educational ministry of youth." To promote its goals and ideals, Catholic education aims to professionalize and integrate its multiple educational apostolates. It is necessary for Catholic education to broaden its base. In addition to providing for Catholic school students, the Catholic school system must also serve Catholic children in public schools and the ever-growing numbers in adult religious education programs.

Learning has long been symbolized by a burning lamp. At times it may seem to be a flickering light. For Catholic education, the lamp continues to burn, lighting new educational visions of learning systems buttressed by educational technology and enriched by a tradition of authentic spiritual formation.

PART I

Why are many catholic schools closing?

If one word were to be used to describe the situation in Catholic education at the present time, the word would probably be *panic*. And panic is never a healthy thing.

In his television series *Civilisation*, Kenneth Clark stated that disillusionment and cynicism are more destructive of civilization than weapons and bombs. He added that when a civilization has gone underground (in the dark ages, for example), the times have always been characterized by a great lack of confidence in the future. Fear can cause wild self-destruction like the apparatus in the television series *Mission Impossible*.

Therefore, although one must be realistic and practical in examining Roman Catholic education in America, one shouldn't be gloomy. Change is engulfing Catholic schools, just as change creeps up on all of us and on our institutions. Catholic educators must meet the challenge of change. This is certainly going to require adjustments. It means we must re-examine our goals and see if we are achieving them. It means we must ask: "Should the American Church remain in the Catholic school business?"

But such questions should be examined with vigor—not despair. Such a self-examination is healthy for all living and maturing organisms. It should indicate life and growth, not destruction and death.

Nothing is to be gained by simply standing around wringing our . hands and moaning. If whole new approaches are required to accomplish today's tasks, if yesterday's forms can no longer do the job, then we must start building new forms.

This is the challenge facing Catholics today.

On June 28, 1971, the United States Supreme Court declared that it was unconstitutional for states to pay teacher salaries in Catholic schools. In an almost unanimous decision the Court strongly warned against excessive entanglement between church and state in America's Catholic schools.

The first question most people now ask concerning Catholic education is: "What's going to happen if Catholic schools continue to close?" It's natural that this would be the most urgent question for parents because often it really means: "What will we do if they close Saint Mary's and Jane can't go there anymore?" To any American not this closely involved it probably means: "What will happen to our taxes if the local Catholic school closes and all those children are thrust into our already over-crowded public schools?"

If I were to say, first of all, that Catholic schools are not going to close, you wouldn't read any further; you'd lose confidence in me immediately. You know that, as a matter of fact, a number of these schools have closed already.

And if you want a perfect prediction of just how many Catholic schools will close (and which ones), I must admit that I have no powers of prophecy. We all know some Catholic schools have already closed, and we know that predicting the future can be hazardous. So what can we do?

The first thing I would suggest is a careful diagnosis. When a doctor attempts to cure a patient he tries to analyze the causes of the ailment. In examining the health of Catholic schools today we must study the changes occurring in the structure. However, we must also ask: What are the underlying causes forcing these structural changes? Why did the decade of the seventies begin with one Catholic school per day closing its doors?[1] Why are some people predicting the demise of Catholic schools by 1975?

Like most medical analyses, the answer isn't a simple one. To say that the problem is chiefly financial is just too pat an answer. Money may be a key consideration, but many other factors are also involved. In this section of this book we'll examine some of them.

EMERGING PATTERNS

The downward trend in Catholic school enrollment has been documented by the historian Harold A. Buetow.[2] Buetow claims that the high point of American Catholic education, in terms of its numbers, was reached about the middle of the nineteen sixties. According to the 1965 *Official Catholic Directory*, there were 6,111,146 students receiving instruction full-time in Catholic schools that year.[3]

The total public school student population in America in 1965 was 42,867,566.[4] Thus, one out of every seven students was educated at that time at the expense of American Catholics, and at no expense to the majority of American taxpayers. Catholics were paying twice to make this possible: they were taxed for public schools and their donations were keeping Catholic schools open. In fact, many other people pay taxes for services they don't use. This logic, however, did not make this load any lighter for American Catholics.

The National Education Association estimates the per pupil cost of educating public school students in 1965 was $454. Thus, during this one school year alone, the cost of educating these Catholic school children would have added almost three billion dollars to the tax bills of American citizens. And every year Catholic schools stayed open, this kind of annual saving to the taxpayer was repeated.

Buetow notes that American Catholics began, about 1965, to cut back on quantity in Catholic education, in order to improve its quality — upgrading teacher qualifications and salaries, and lowering class size.

We now see a new pattern emerging.

Enrollments below college level decreased 4.3 percent for 1967-68, and another 5 percent for the 1968-1969 school year.[5] Thus, the seventies began, as we've noted, with a clear pattern of "closings."

The NEA records that the average cost of educating a pupil in the public schools has increased annually so the 1971-72 cost was almost double the 1965 per pupil expense ($867 instead of $454).[6] Each Catholic school student moving into a public school adds this amount to the public's tax responsibility. From 1965 to 1972, American taxpayers have already paid over one billion dollars in additional taxes to cover the cost of absorbing pupils from Catholic schools that have closed.

Year	Decrease in Catholic School Enrollment		NEA Per-Pupil Cost (Average)		Cost to American Taxpayers (EACH YEAR)
1966	56,586	x	$507	=	$ 28,689,102
1967	100,699	x	538	=	54,176,062
1968	217,187	x	594	=	129,009,074
1969	225,624	x	655	=	147,783,720
1970	323,727	x	722	=	233,730,894
1971	297,705	x	812	=	241,736,460
1972	364,171	x	867	=	315,736,257

Total DECREASE in Catholic School Enrollment, 1966-1972   1,585,699

Total COST TO AMERICAN TAXPAYERS $1,150,861,569.00

(Over one billion dollars)

Thus, the tax increase total from 1966 through 1972 was $1,150,861,-569. Obviously, Catholic school closings have affected the pocketbook of all American citizens, whatever religious affiliation they profess. As this is written, public schools face staggering financial problems. This reality, however, is worsened by each Catholic school's demise.

It is ironic that, historically, the Catholic school system in America witnessed a veritable explosion of growth up to 1965.

Before World War I, with the arrival of vast numbers of immigrants, the Roman Catholic Church rose to relative power and prestige in America. In 1890 there were only eight million Catholics in this country. In thirty years (by 1920), there were almost eighteen million American Catholics. Thus, in thirty years, the Catholic population more than doubled.

After World War I, the enrollment in Catholic schools tripled within forty years.[7] In 1917 there were 1,537,644 students in Catholic schools. By 1957 these schools enrolled 4,300,000 young people. [8] And, as we have noted, at its peak, in 1965, the American Catholic school system was educating over six million students.

Buetow's growth analysis and recent statistical studies issued by the national Catholic Educational Association provide dramatic contrasts. NCEA figures recently documented a 10 percent enrollment decline over a two-year period. The 1971-72 school year alone showed an 8 percent drop in elementary school enrollment and a 5.4 percent drop in enrollments in Catholic secondary schools. As the decade of the seventies dawned, the Catholic Church was investing 1.4 billion dollars annually in its school program.[9]

Thus, as enrollments were decreasing, *annual* operating costs for Catholic schools increased by more than 200 million dollars over the 1965 figures.

STATISTICS TRANSLATED INTO HUMAN LIVES

Figures of declining Catholic school enrollments form a significant part of our story, but the facts are much more complex. The downward numerical trend has had many repercussions, and the general public is gradually becoming aware of them.

The most important impact of this trend was its effect on people. Statistics can be bare and boring; but human beings and the pain they feel — these things are very real and personal.

Many parents were faced with the sad, but very necessary decision of removing their children with regret from Catholic schools as the tuition rates went beyond their means. Many of these parents were themselves the products of Catholic schools, and this meant a break with a tradition that may have gone back several generations. However, it was the only decision open to many.

Some parents who actually wanted to continue sacrificing to pay high tuitions did not have the choice. Many parishioners learned suddenly on a Sunday morning (or read in a daily newspaper) that the decision had been made to close their parochial school—it simply couldn't carry on any longer financially. This often created turmoil in the lives of the families involved, and also raised many legitimate questions about why the people who pay were not part of this decision-making process.

Some of the suffering has been felt by those who staffed the schools also. Occasionally, a religious order had built up a half century or more of service in one particular parish. When this tie was broken, it meant more than a little sadness. Much history and tradition end with such closings.

The economic impact of Catholic school closings meant that the pain was not limited to Catholics. Many taxpayers were hurt as the effect of a school closing was felt in forcing local taxes upward.

With the aid of teaching sisters and brothers who received a small salary, Catholic schools had been able to keep the cost of educating individual students much below the per-pupil cost in public schools. For example, in 1969-70, it cost an average of $722 per pupil to educate a child in a public school. During that same school year, the Catholic-school per-pupil cost was only $200 in elementary schools, although the high school cost was somewhat higher.[10]

Thus, on the average it cost $722 that year to educate a student in a public school. This figure does vary from community to community, of course. A wealthy suburb will spend more on its schools than a middle-class or inner-city area would. It's easy to figure that if a city or town is spending $722 per pupil on education the bill is increased in just one year almost $200,000 if a Catholic school closes forcing 252 students into the local public school system. (This figure would go higher if the public school must also build new classrooms for the new students.) This increase is reflected in ever-rising tax rates. Taxpayers — both Catholic and non-Catholic — begin to complain. (It is difficult to assess these increased costs absolutely accurately. Some Catholic-school students may occupy seats that were empty in public schools. However, even in this case, the overhead educational costs would be increased.)

Mini-billboards advertising tax savings went up in front of Catholic schools in Illinois. One sign read: "TAXPAYER'S BEST FRIEND — This Non-Public School Saves Illinois taxpayers $138,840 annually (267 pupils x $520 minimum state aid, plus $291,000 building cost)."[11]

These economic facts are behind a dramatic switch in America's public opinion concerning aid to Catholic schools. The United States Supreme Court did not consider this in their 1971 decision against direct aid. (As a matter of fact, the Court indicated that approval of such aid would lead to bitter battles in state legislatures. In fact, however, most Americans now favor such aid.) As far back as June,1969, the *New York*

Times referred to a movement "gaining momentum throughout the nation."[12] The article cited growing support for giving Catholic schools financial aid. The survey noted that the old church-state argument was now overshadowed by the economic argument that it may be cheaper to aid parochial school pupils now than to take on the further cost burden if these schools are forced to close.

The power of these arguments also began to cause an important breakthrough in the long standing aid-to-schools protest on the part of nearly every important segment in the Jewish community. The New York Board of Rabbis, representing more than one thousand rabbis in the metropolitan New York area, stated: "The insistence that those involved (in parochial education) carry the full financial burden themselves has become increasingly unrealistic in the contemporary economy."[13]

Other factors have probably contributed to this dramatic about-face in public opinion. The personalities of Pope John XXIII and President John Kennedy seemed to make Catholics in general more acceptable and less suspect. And the open debate within the Roman Catholic Church during the Vatican Council and following it seemed to reassure non-Catholics that the Church was making an honest effort to modernize itself. So, after experiencing a Catholic President and witnessing the beginning of ecumenical understanding, many non-Catholic Americans seemed more agreeable to the idea of public funds for private school pupils. It still remains most probable, however, that what changed people's minds more than anything else was the extremely practical knowledge that with every Catholic school closing the tax bills went up.

This economic factor began to spill over into the political arena. Politicians are very sensitive to practical matters like increased taxes. Thus, nationally and locally, political leaders began urging the government to do something about the fact that Catholic schools were in serious trouble.

At the highest level, nationally, this action took the form of two special commissions.[14]

In 1972, in fact, two significant government commissions provided statistics and insights concerning the total American school finance crisis. Covered were the problems and potential of public, as well as non-public schools.

The first report, *Schools, People, and Money: The Need for Educational Reform*, was submitted to President Nixon by the Commission on School Finance. This report deals with the entire financial structure of education in America. Covered are topics such as: strengthening state funding and administration of education; saving inner city schools; the public interest in nonpublic education; accountability; innovations; and career needs. The basic theme of the report is the need for reform in the area of American education and school finance.

16

The second report was submitted by a four-member panel (or subcommittee) of the above commission on school finance. The report of this special panel is entitled *Nonpublic Education and the Public Good*. The report concludes that, viewed within the interests of our entire educational system, nonpublic school enrollments are falling and costs are climbing. They added: "The trends, however, are neither inexorable nor inevitable if certain initiatives are undertaken." The commission warned, however, "if the decline continues, pluralism in education will cease, [and] parental options will virtually terminate . . . ."

Such commission reports, of course, do not determine policy, but they often guide it. Both studies are based upon the latest research and statistics, since the panels contracted for these studies while preparing their analyses.

A brief analysis of each report will be helpful.

The earliest report gives a background or context for the later one on nonpublic education. It is, therefore, valuable to study the broad need for educational reform in public education before moving to the challenge of America's nonpublic schools.

The President's Commission on School Finance muses that "for millions of children, American education—both public and nonpublic—is not working as it was intended to work." However, the commission feels "the present educational system is basically sound. What is needed is not its rejection, but its improvement...we must alter many parts of our American educational structure, but as we rebuild, we shall do well to protect its foundations, for they are solid."

The commission noted among its major findings:

The financial problems of education derive largely from the evolving inabilities of the states to create and maintain systems that provide equal educational opportunities and quality education to all their children.

The conviction that class size has an important or even a measurable effect on educational quality cannot presently be supported by evidence.

The survival of Catholic schools does not depend totally or even mainly on the amount of money available to them. We do not agree with those who argue that money is the remedy for virtually all the ills of our educational system.

The report challenges that "interrelationships among the governments, institutions, and people—complex and intractable as they appear—must and, in fact, do provide means for reform."

Major recommendations of the commission for implementing such reform include:

1. Wider use of each state's instrumentalities.
   (The commission sees the federal government offering leadership and a pioneering role, but only a supplementary role to the states in school financing. It recommends strengthening state administrations of education.)
2. Full state funding of elementary and secondary education, with differentials based on educational need, and supported by general purpose federal incentive grants.
3. A five-year plan to save inner city schools, called an Urban Educational Assistance Program.
4. The adoption of programs of early childhood education commencing at age 4.
5. An endorsement of financial aid to nonpublic schools.
   (The commission recommends that local, state and federal funds be used to provide, where constitutionally permissible, public benefits for nonpublic school children. The group endorsed the tax credit concept, as well as other aid formulas.)
6. More accountability of school fund uses.
7. Career education, given priority and status at least equal to that now accorded to college preparation.
8. Reorganization of school districts, to attain diversity and to reduce disparities.
9. Government support for experimentation and innovation.
10. Considerable increases in federal outlays in education.
    (The commission warns, however, "we have seen the need to tie these outlays to reform.")
11. General revenue sharing and welfare reform.
12. The establishment of a National Institute of Education—to provide additional research in how children learn, how technology influences learning, and new modes of providing education.

Clarence Walton, a commission member, offered a discerning comment and warning. He called attention to the permeating philosophy of the report; namely, "that states hold primacy in the education of children. What no commissioner specifically asserts, many seem implicitly to accept. I hold that the primary responsibility for the child's education rests with the parent. I hold that too much benign neglect of the parent's role already exists and that steps should be taken to halt it!"

Before moving to the next report by the nonpublic school panel, it would be helpful to study the view of nonpublic education as it is reflected in this first overall financial report. The Commission on School Finance—studying financial problems of both public and nonpublic schools—notes that nonpublic schools serve a public purpose by providing diversity, choice and healthy competition to traditional public education. The commission adds that nonpublic schools "provide the means for a substantial group of Americans to express themselves socially, ethically, culturally, and religiously through educational institutions."

Citing increased public school operating costs if nonpublic schools close, the commission estimates the total increase "might run from as low as about $1.3 billion to as high as $3.2 billion and the cost of building new facilities would range from $4.7 billion to just short of $10 billion."

The commission also notes that "closing of urban nonpublic schools can damage not only already decaying public schools, but also increase the racial isolation of inner city neighborhoods."

Concluding that "there are permissable ways of providing public aid to children who happen to be enrolled in nonpublic schools," the commission urges tax credits, tax deductions for tuition, tuition reimbursement, scholarship aid based on need, and equitable sharing in federally supported assistance programs.

These recommendations provide a background for an analysis of *Nonpublic Education and the Public Good*, the second Presidential commission report. In an accompanying letter to President Nixon, Clarence Walton, the Chairman of the President's Panel on Nonpublic Education, warns: "The next few years are critical to the future of pluralism in education. Whatever is done must be undertaken with a profound sense of urgency."

Walton's letter also hints at the dual thrust of the report: "Nonpublic schools need and deserve outside help, [but] large efforts of self-help are also required."

Noting alarming enrollment decreases in nonpublic schools, the commission draws three major conclusions:

1. Public schools least able to accommodate additional pupils would be the ones generally hardest hit by the tide of transfers from closing nonpublic schools.

2. Municipalities, already heavily burdened with rising taxes for projected public education needs, would confront militant demands for even higher tax rates to sustain crowded public schools.

3. Social costs may prove to be even higher than economic ones. For larger cities, closing nonpublic schools would have a marked impact on housing patterns, unemployment ratios, and racial stability.

The commission lists special recommendations for supporters of nonpublic schools, as part of the self-help called for above. It urged the nonpublic school community to: sharpen identity by defining specific goals and objectives for schools; associate with public and other nonpublic agencies; practice accountability; break the problem-psychosis syndrome; recruit vigorously; experiment with mobile construction; mount public relations projects; control operating costs; reach out to private income sources; build partnerships with colleges and universities; involve parents; and be a dedicated partner in integrated education.

Commission recommendations for the general public include a federal assistance program for the urban poor, federal income tax credits to parents, a federal construction loan program, and tuition reimbursements.

The commission report, *Nonpublic Education and the Public Good*, also includes an in-depth analysis of tax credits, as well as an historical survey of the complex issues of constitutional law. These constitutional criteria provide guidelines for financial aid programs to nonpublic schools.

These presidential commission reports, studied together, provide a context for understanding the Catholic school problem, since 83 percent of all American nonpublic schools are Catholic schools. The reports analyze the existing facts, and draw reform conclusions from these facts. To use a current phrase, the reports reflect "a blueprint for action."

In his educational message to Congress on March 3, 1970, the President said: "The government cannot be indifferent to the potential collapse of its private and parochial schools." The President added that the absence of competition in education would neither be good for the public school system nor good for the country. [15] Earlier, in Pittsburgh, on October 28, 1968, Nixon had stated: "It would be a tragedy of the first magnitude if private schools were driven out of existence." [16]

President Nixon made the following public commitments and statements before almost 1500 Catholic educators meeting in Philadelphia, in the spring of 1972:

> *America needs her nonpublic schools. These nonpublic schools need help. Therefore, we must and will find ways to provide that help. The legislative recommendations which we finally submit will be equitable, will be workable, will be constitutional and so held by the Supreme Court.*

Mr. Nixon reminded Americans that nonpublic schools in this country educate more children than the public school system of the whole state of California, or the public school system of the whole state of New York. After citing increased costs to American taxpayers if these schools are forced to close ($3 billion annually in operating costs, and $10 billion in new school construction), the President commented:

> For many Americans, allegiance to their nonpublic community schools is their strongest and sometimes, perhaps, their only single tie to city life. If their schools should close, many of these families would abandon the city and go to the suburbs. This, in turn, would further worsen the racial isolation of our central cities—a development we must not permit.

Then, after economic and political pressure, came legal pressure. State legislators began pushing for laws to make aid to Catholic schools possible. In Ohio, Rhode Island, Connecticut and New York, legislatures approved aid to private schools. And political leaders from both parties began to discuss amending state constitutions to make aid possible. The issue of state aid to parochial and private schools was introduced in at least thirty-one state legislatures in 1969. [17]

The most significant legal impact, however, was reserved for our highest court. The Supreme Court of the United States agreed to hear cases concerning the constitutionality of the legislation in Pennsylvania, Connecticut and Rhode Island. [18]

Thus, the personal, economic and political impact of the closing of many Catholic schools resulted in a new Supreme Court guideline decision. This high court ruling clarified the position of the United States Constitution concerning the use of public money for nonpublic schools, according to current Supreme Court interpretations.

And, as we noted at the beginning of this book, pure panic resulted when the Supreme Court strongly opposed the growing acceptance of direct aid to Catholic schools, ruling against payment of teacher salaries in these schools with public funds.

FACTORS FORCING CHANGE

If we sat around your kitchen table, armed with cups of coffee, and tried to come up with a list of causes for Catholic school closings, some underlying developments and trends would enter our discussion.

1. Increased dependence upon lay teachers.
   Every time you replace a nun with a lay teacher, the Catholic school budget takes a big jump. A sister's salary in 1969, for example, might be $2200 per year. [19] A lay teacher stepping into the same classroom might be paid five, six, or seven thousand dollars. [20] For a medium-sized parish to add five or six lay teachers to its staff will add between twenty-five and fifty thousand dollars a year to its budget. Parish income is not

increasing proportionally; as a matter of fact, parish income is decreasing, even as school costs increase.

2. Changes occurring in religious orders staffing Catholic schools. The development of Catholic schools in America has been intimately connected with the religious orders staffing these schools. Any major changes in these religious communities directly affect Catholic schools. Such a major change occurred after the Vatican Council and is still in process. "The New Nuns" will be discussed later in this section of the book.

3. The changing character of the Catholic population in America. Historically, American Catholics have existed within a defensive church structure, a type of protective ghetto. This reflected the immigrant background of most Catholics and their consequent lack of education and professional status. Today, Catholics do as well economically and socially as other Americans. They are no longer a ghetto group.

4. The general re-evaluation of Catholic goals inspired by the Vatican Council.
As the Church moved into the sixties and the seventies, Catholics began to ask themselves just what their priorities should be. Questions arose. Are we pouring too much money into Catholic schools and neglecting all those Catholic youth who are not in those schools but, instead, attend public schools and colleges? And people even began to ask about educating the adults who aren't in school. Should we be providing more programs for adults with our money, instead of pouring it into Catholic schools serving less than one-half of our youth?

5. Changes in society.
With the scientific revolution producing rapid change in our world, and with young people reflecting their unique rebellion, it is more difficult for traditional Catholic educators to be relevant to young people in our television-dominated nuclear age. Students making their own decisions now may ask: "Who needs it?" (a Catholic education, that is.)

6. Theological factors.
As the Roman Catholic Church constantly re-examines her theology and philosophy, this probing and questioning will be reflected in her academic institutions. A key question facing the Church is what attitude should she adopt toward the secular, as opposed to the sacred. Should churches protect people from the dangers of the secular world? Or is this playing ostrich—burying heads in the sand? Rather, should churches expose people to the realities of the world's problems in an attempt to help people solve these problems? Should religious orders in the Church

focus on contemplation and prayer primarily, or should they be social action oriented? Should the Church place concern with the "here" as a priority higher than "the hereafter"? And should we even separate the concepts of "the Church" and "the people"? Isn't it true that the people ARE the Church?

These are some of the Catholic educational challenges we could uncover at our coffee klatch. They summarize the key factors currently at work weakening the structure of Catholic schools in America. This is, however, just a summary. We must explore the consequences of these challenges.

To lay a foundation for our exploration of causes, let's begin with a look at a typical troubled parish budget. This will give us a practical example of the specific problems facing many American Catholic parishes at the present time.

FINANCIAL WOES

Parents know better than most people that the cost of living is going up these days. Just as it's almost impossible to balance the budget in many American homes, the Catholic educational budget is in very serious trouble in many American parishes.

Pouring over cost-analysis sheets is for the professional accountant. However, lay people are supposed to have more and more responsibility for leadership in the Roman Catholic Church today. And, after all, they are the ones who pay the bills. So it is good to become aware of Catholic education's financial facts of life.

The best way to do this is to break down a school budget and examine it. Fortunately, this is becoming easier for us, because many Catholic administrators are making their financial reports available. This is good for the Church leaders, as well as the laity. Lay people can be sympathetic about the Church's financial woes only if they have the facts.

There are three varieties of Catholic schools in America and the financial picture for each type of school is a little different.

The Catholic school most parents are familiar with is the local *parish school*. In the past, this school has always been supported by the members of an individual parish, or congregation. St. Mark's parish, for example, might have a large inner-city church, and might support both an elementary school and high school. Such parish schools were built originally to provide a Catholic education for the children who resided within the parish boundaries.

The second category of Catholic school is the *diocesan school*. As its name suggests, the diocesan school is supported by the whole diocese, not by just one parish. Many diocesan schools are large high schools, which, with their modern science labs and language lab equipment, are so costly that a single parish could hardly afford to build and maintain one. With the entire diocese underwriting the cost, however, the school can serve commuting students from many cities or towns within the diocese. This school, as you have probably guessed, is very similar to the "regional high school" so familiar in public school edcuation.

The third type of Catholic school is the *private academy*. This school is legally owned by a specific religious community, like the Dominican Sisters, or the Jesuits, and is financed and administered by the religious order. The private school does not exist to serve a particular parish and is not financed by the parish. The diocese has no direct control over its finances either. Of course, private schools exist within the geographical boundaries of a diocese and, strictly speaking, such an academy is subject to diocesan educational regulations.

Now—due to the financial woes besetting all three types of Catholic schools—a rather confusing thing is happening. Many schools are moving from one category into another. More and more parish schools are becoming diocesan schools, because the parish needs financial help from the diocese to keep its school going. And many parish schools are consolidating, so one school can serve several parishes at the same time, a type of inter-parish school.

Diocesan schools have another variant too. For example, in the inner city, or in a major city, a parish school might be almost deserted financially, as the Catholic residents move out to the suburbs. What do you do with the school building then? In some cases, the Church can perform a real service to the inner city if the school is kept open to help deprived youngsters who need special educational attention. This also provides an educational alternative for concerned inner-city parents who deserve a choice as much as parents with more income do. Many inner-city schools cannot be supported by the existing local parish because that parish simply doesn't exist as it did years ago with a large Catholic population. In this case the diocese sometimes subsidizes the educational operation of the parish school, making it, in effect, a diocesan school.

Some experts feel that eventually most Catholic schools should be run and financed by the whole diocese, or some other regional administrative body. [21]

In *Public Monies for Nonpublic Schools?*, Professor Ernest Bartell, C.S.C., of Notre Dame University, notes: "In Ohio, the diocese ... costs were a meager $65 per pupil in 1958, they had gone up to $92 . . . by 1963, and were up to about $200 per pupil in 1969. Three hundred percent increases over a ten-year period are fairly typical in the operating cost of Catholic schools."

When a pastor and parish council meet to discuss the details of budget figures, a key question is bound to be: "How long can this parish continue to support a Catholic school without outside assistance?"

"IF OUR FATHERS COULD DO IT . . ."

Another significant question we might ask is "Why is the typical American Catholic parish having trouble supporting a school today in an affluent America, if American Catholics could support and expand these schools when Catholics were not as well off financially in the past?" If immigrants on low salaries could do it, why can't Catholics do it today?

This financial problem is tied directly to the presence of lay teachers in Catholic schools today. In past years, an immigrant Catholic population was able to support the Catholic-school system primarily because the teachers in these schools received the incredibly low salaries paid to nuns at that time. These sisters, brothers and priests were especially dedicated to the concept of a Catholic school and literally donated their services as part of an apostolic program that has few equals historically, in terms of service. This donated service was probably the most significant aspect of Catholic education in the past. The system simply couldn't have expanded and matured without it.

When lay teachers began working in Catholic schools along with the teachers from the religious orders, costs began their upward trend. Lay teachers do not live in a convent, with the parish paying a percentage of their living expenses; the lay teacher needs a living wage.

A unique exception might provide one key to Catholic school financial problems. In St. Kevin's Parish, Dorchester, Massachusetts, Father Joseph Kierce, advertised for "Volunteer Corps" applicants. Candidates would teach for one dollar a day plus room and board, or they could choose to receive $49.00 per week. This pastor assured me he had a very good response and filled vacancies easily with qualified teachers.

A friend of mine has often commented that the Church isn't demanding heroic sacrifices anymore and many people want to offer just that. This experience seems to indicate he may be right. A pastor referring to a special case of inflated faculty salaries, noted in a major urban newspaper: "Recently in the Boston *Globe* it was reported that in St. James, Haverhill, (Massachusetts) one lay teacher was employed in 1961. (Religious and lay teacher) salaries that year were approximately $20,000. In seven years in that parish, salary costs have more than quadrupled; salaries at St. James will consume $90,000 this year (1968). Any pastor who has to pay $90,000 each year in teacher salaries has financial headaches of migraine proportions!"[22]

Of course, increased building and maintenance costs have contributed to these headaches. The principal of St. Mary's High School in Waltham, Massachusetts, writing in the same newspaper, also called attention to this fact. He noted that a survey indicated a building costing $170,000 forty years ago would be built in 1968 at a cost of $900,000. And imagine what inflation has added to the cost since then!

To be honest, we must realize that there can be a question of whether schools were cheaper then in terms of constant "real-purchasing-power" dollars. Or in terms of a worker's weekly income. One commentator recently told me: "I strongly suspect that our grandfathers gave a larger percentage of their small earnings to the Church and schools than we do of our larger incomes now."

All these factors must be considered if one is to grumble loudly: "If poor immigrants could support a separate school system, why can't today's Catholics continue to carry the burden without some complaints and outside help?"

THE NEW NUNS

Financial facts, like the ones covered in the preceding section, are fairly easy to analyze and dissect. Current surveys clearly show the trend toward more lay teachers in Catholic schools, with both advantages and disadvantages, educationally and fiscally.

A much more complex topic is the second factor we listed in connection with Catholic school closings: changes occurring within the religious orders staffing these schools.

What transpires behind the closed doors of a convent has always been a mystery to most people, often a most appealing and intriguing mystery. To those looking at the religious community through youthful eyes, the nun often seemed awe-inspiring, but staid. Many, of course, were warm, humble, modest, and well-disciplined—qualities many people still respect. Often, however, a sister would not emerge strongly as a person because of her strict adherence to her religious congregation's standards of dress and thought.

Now, through the window-pane of Vatican II, we see a new type of religious woman emerging. This nun appears to have individuality and color. Most obvious, of course, is the change in clothing. The old dress styles were called "habits" by those who wore them. Hemlines have come up, veils have come off; many brothers and sisters wear simple business suits. Within the same religious congregation we may see many modes of dress.

What to many Catholics was order, now seems unbearable chaos. However, out of this apparent disorder could emerge a new religious, a new person, who finds that instead of being apart from the world, she can now respond and relate to all people in a truly Christian attitude of service. Those whom we, as lay people, address as "sister" can become even more worthy of that title within the human family.

Many religious communities of women were established centuries ago. It is bound to be quite a jolt to the congregation's structure and personnel when significant changes are made in a pattern of living that has become hallowed as the group's holy tradition.

Thus, the "generation gap" we are all so familiar with in our own lives found its way behind convent walls. One of the greatest challenges facing most nuns as adaptation progressed became this one: How do you reconcile the older sister with her youthful counterpart? One woman may have given forty years of dedicated service in Catholic schools; her formation and training might have stressed humility and complete abdication of self. The young sister came into the convent from a world where she had much freedom and individuality; her formation within the convent was more open and less strict than that of the older sister.

The new approach features *self-determination* as well. Sisters are now encouraged to select their own assignments instead of being told where they will be sent to work.

Occasionally, problems arose when these two types of women would try to restructure their congregation's rule for living. Even changing her habit of dress might be difficult for the older nun. If these women were to be truly kind to each other, however, love would demand that each one listen to the needs of the other and try to rebuild a life bearable for both.

The changing outward appearance of today's nun reflects deeper changes in the theology of religious life. Since the Vatican Council many people have been analyzing the whole concept of living together in a community of service to the Church and the world. For the purposes of this book we must take some time to reflect on these innovations. The future of the Catholic school system in America seems quite intimately tied to the future of religious orders. When nuns change, or when lay teachers replace nuns, there is the possibility of a "crisis of confidence" in Catholic schools. And, as we have noted, the Catholic school system probably would never have been built in the first place without the dedicated existence of such religious personnel.

An article in *Harper's* noted that while the total value of the contributed services of sisters is pure speculation, some indication can be found in their major area of activity, the schools. More than 100,000 sisters in education could account for as much as one-half of the total $2 billion estimated annual contributed value of the U.S. Catholic educational enterprise. [23] The case may be somewhat overstated here, but it's easy to see the role that dedicated religious personnel have played historically. Dr. George Elford, Research Director of NCEA notes a conservative estimate of the contributed services of religious in 1971 alone, was 340 million dollars.

This section is entitled "The New Nuns" because the vast majority of individuals within religious orders staffing American Catholic schools have always been female. There are, however, others involved. The 1960s opened with 160,632 full-time teachers in Catholic schools. [24] There were 98,471 sisters among that total. 10,890 priests were also full-time teachers in 1960. These numbers were augmented by 4,778 teaching brothers. (The term "brother" is used to designate a man who is not ordained a priest, but who desires to make a special commitment to serve.) In 1960, 45,506 lay teachers served in Catholic schools also.

As the decade closed the personnel pattern was shifting. In 1969, the total number of Catholic school teachers reached 204,957. The largest group consisted of lay teachers: 95,363. There were 92,718 sisters, 10,980 priests, and 5,291 brothers among that total. For the first time lay teachers outnumbered any other single group teaching in Catholic schools.

As we begin to analyze changes occurring within religious orders we must remember that many of these changes affected priests and brothers, along with nuns. We refer to nuns generally, but the basic factors apply to all those dedicated by special vows to the religious life.

THE MEANING OF "COMMUNITY"

Each one of us lives in a community. It could be a small town or a section of a large metropolitan area. It could be a community of geographical, financial, or social bonds. It could be both or several. The one adhesive factor making it a community is the grouping together of individuals for a common purpose. Our entire national population actually consists of a grouping of small communities. And the phrase "the family of man" refers to a broad-based community concept of the whole world. (Many religious educators say the chief goal of Catholic education today should be "building Faith Communities.")

The Roman Cahtolic Church is a spiritual community, composed of smaller groups of people banded together for the fulfillment of a common goal. In the history of this Church we see the formation of many communities of religious men and women, with specialized spiritual goals.

Just as any chemical or biological structure must have some organization for stability, so, too, must any community of man. For this reason men make laws to govern and control the operation of a community. The religious commune is no different. Thus, communal structures develop.

Naturally, the term community loses much of its vitality if the group working together is merely a legalistic structure without the real bond based on love and shared goals. For just this reason, many religious communities are involved in a soul-searching re-examination of their structure and their goals. In some cases the organizational bureaucracy of the religious community has received more attention than the real human needs of the members working in common. Rigid codes and static systems dehumanize people. Religious congregations are beginning to become more democratic and open and free; thus, a real sense of community can return to the individual and to the group. Such a "Faith Community" model can serve the parish as well.

This leads to the crucial challenge facing religious communities as they conduct their own "examination of conscience." The groups find themselves asking various questions:

- • • How much structure is necessary to work well together?

- • • Can individuals retain a degree of freedom and still operate as an integral part of the whole group? (This is similar to many a married woman's quandry: How do I learn to put my family first, and—at the same time—retain my own individuality and identity?)

- • • Is the goal of private prayer a practical or meaningful one in a technological society? Or, is it possible that contemplation is more necessary than ever, given the fast pace of modern man?

- • • Can such communities be relevant if they do not become involved in modern man's problems, problems such as poverty and racial injustice?

- • • Is it necessary for individuals to remain celibate within such groups? Can communities of married couples and families survive, or are there too many theological and human relations problems involved?

- • • Can today's religious community offer a "theology of witness"—an example for the modern world? (One dramatic example would be the "Convent of Atonement" at Dachau. Here Carmelite nuns pray almost continuously for the souls of all who were martyred there.)

- • • Will the religious community of the future be small and personal, instead of the large groups we now know?

In exploring these complex questions concerning religious communities in America today, I am not offering solutions; I am merely trying to clarify some of the concepts involved. (It would be presumptous to say I have the answers; I have never even lived within a religious community's structure. I have done extensive study on the subject; and over the last ten years of working closely with members of religious communities, I have had many talks with those who are intimately involved with the changes occurring within these communities. I am trying here to reflect their insights.)

Most of the books written on the philosophical and theological concepts of relgous community were written for the consumption of the community members themselves. This is understandable since they are the ones most intimately involved in these basic discussions. However, since these changes are having far-reaching effects upon the Church and her school system in America, parents ought to know what is happening.

THE BIRTH OF RELIGIOUS COMMUNITIES

To understand the complexities of today's scene we must go back into an age that doesn't seem quite as complicated as our own. If we return to the first few centuries of the Christian Church, we can examine the early growth of Christian religious communities. Incidentally, it is interesting to see that man's devotion to God often seems to be linked to the concept of groups being set apart or especially dedicated to paying homage to God continually. It is fascinating, too, to note that monastic practice actually precedes Christianity.

In its broadest sense, monasticism means a way of life characterized by seclusion and withdrawal from society. Generally this is done by individuals seeking to elevate the human soul to perfection of virtue and to union with God.

Most people reading about gurus today will recognize that there have been monastic practices in Buddhism and Islam. Similar, too, were the Jewish Essenes who existed before Christ. The vestal virgins of the Roman Empire were set apart for a specified period of time as a community to perform religious functions.

Christian monasticism had its origins in the deserts of Egypt. An early name associated with this development is St. Basil the Great (330-379 A.D.). Basil (sounding very contemporary) said fasting and penance should not interfere with work itself, and he urged that monastic life be completely isolated from society and its problems.

Although monasticism had an Eastern background originally, it soon spread to the West. The man who Westernized monasticism lived from 480 to approximately 550 A.D. and his name was Benedict of Nursia.

St. Benedict was disturbed by the lack of morality in society in general, so he withdrew to a cave near Rome at the beginning of the sixth century to live as a hermit. Gradually, as other men wanted to follow his example and joined him, he established monasteries, the most famous being Monte Cassino.

Over a period of years, Benedict developed a number of rules to guide these men. *The Rule of St. Benedict* is a classic document in Church history and set the pattern of monastic life for men and women which prevailed in the West for nearly six centuries. Benedict said the aims of good works were to "relieve the poor" and "to help the afflicted." [25]

Benedict's approach to government was quite modern when you consider that he was developing his code approximately fifteen centuries ago. He wrote that the community should be called into council for advice to the abbot on important matters. The principles of Benedict's Rule were flexible enough to provide guidelines for many religious orders established centuries later with a variety of apostolates. As the seventies dawned the Benedictines alone consisted of 2,007 priests and 562 brothers.[26]

The thirteenth century saw a new approach to religious life. Man now moved among the population and depended upon alms for a living. The name of St. Francis of Assisi comes to mind in connection with such friars.

The Jesuit order was born in the sixteenth century, and The Catholic Almanac notes that the Sisters of Charity, in 1633, were the first community of women with simple vows to gain Church approval. The many varieties of religious communities which developed since have not been restricted to the life style of the early monks on the Egyptian deserts. Later communities moved into education, health and social service, communications, and many other fields.

ARE RELIGIOUS ORDERS RELEVANT TODAY?

A recent writer suggested that in a country where people sit on floor mats, a chair manufacturer must change the whole society before he can expect to sell chairs.[27] Likewise, as society changes, religious communities must change if the concept of religious life is to be "bought" by prospective candidates to this life style.

As the expression goes, "a lot of water has passed under the bridge" since the early days of monasticism, or even since the late Middle Ages. St. Francis and his friars walked the earth many centuries before our vast scientific revolution with its electric power, automation, television sets, and its theory of relativity.

St. Benedict and his monks never heard of Sigmund Freud and all the complex psychological concepts he was to propose about the human personality. Such men couldn't have even conceived of a "new world"—an American nation that would give all churches a unique experiment in church-state relations. Monks were unfamiliar with democratic practice as we know it today. Monastic leaders understood the concept of democracy in early Greece and Rome. St. Benedict shared his authority; however, the political life of the Middle Ages revolved around kings and nobles, contrasted with serfs.

Most of the founders of the great religious orders left behind them rules to govern these congregations, just as Benedict did. And these rules have been followed within the orders with very few changes while the world outside was being revolutionized by science, economics, and politics.

You may wonder how a religious community could remain relatively unchanged century after century, and still be relevant or meaningful in new eras. Well, frankly, this is the very question many religious communities have been forced to ask themselves since the Vatican Council.

As a matter of fact, soul-searching began in religious life before the second Vatican Council. In the area of professional preparation, such renewal received its impetus from an educational standards movement known as "Sister-Formation."

Sister Formation was indirectly launched by an earlier Pope. In 1951, Pope Pius XII urged the first International Congress of Teaching Sisters to insist upon the highest professional standards for all religious groups engaged in education and social work. In 1953 the Sister Formation Conference became an official branch of the National Catholic Educational Association.

The sisters themselves wanted to up-grade their own education and professional competence. It was well known that many of the sisters teaching in Catholic schools did not have a college degree. The dynamic growth of the school system caused priests and bishops to cry out for more and more nuns to staff more and more schools. Consequently, many young girls barely finished their brief spiritual training as novices before they found themselves in classrooms with students in front of them. Then, summer after summer would be spent working for their college degree.

Many public school teachers, years ago, did not have a college degree, as we know it, either. But that did not make the non-degreed nuns feel any better about their lack of professional training. And, of course, the *exclusive* use of degreed personnel in public schools preceded the same educational reform in the Catholic school system.

The Jesuit Rev. Neil G. McCluskey summarizes the new Sister Formation approach known as "the Everett Plan" because it grew out of a workshop held in Everett, Washington in the summer of 1956: "According to the Everett plan, the period of training called the postulate corresponds to the freshman year of college, and the two-year novitiate is to include the so-called canonical year of novitiate and a second year of college. It might be recalled that since the Church-required canonical year is devoted mainly to religious formation, a novice cannot carry a full academic load. The fourth and fifth years are the full junior and senior years of college. The basic curriculum leads to the Bachelor of Arts degree with concentration in the humanities and social sciences. Ideally the five-year Everett curriculum is to be taught in a special kind of college—the "juniorate" —or the equivalent of the seminary. This is simply recognition that sister education has to be college education with something else."[28]

The Sister Formation movement helped the modern nun take some pride in her own person because it gave her the professional competence the times demand. Then another renewal revolution began during the Vatican Council.

In 1965, Pope Paul VI issued a "Decree on the Adaptation and Renewal of Religious Life".[29] In this document, the Holy Father specified that for religious communities the manner of living, praying and working should be adapted to the physical, psychological, cultural, social, and economical circumstances of our age. He said obsolete laws should be eliminated. He urged religious superiors to let members of the community participate in significant decisions affecting the whole community. He said monastic life should be preserved, but he added that adjustments should be made in rules and customs to fit the specific demands of the tasks to be performed. He reminded religious communities to avoid luxury and excessive wealth. And he said that religious habits should be "simple, and modest, poor and . . . becoming."

These pleas by the Pope called countless committees into being within religious communities to up-date dress, structures and forms. One nun said to me, many meetings later: "I'm being dialogued to death!"

New factors emerged in a nun's life, in addition to her new self-determination. She now had new apostolates open to her. And she could serve—in new ways—as a witness within the religious community.

To get a clearer idea of what is involved here, let's use an analogy. Suppose you've just bought a house. However, it's old and it needs some repair work.

You begin with the roof and a paint job. These things are quite obvious, and you feel this repair work will really make a big difference in the appearance of the house. However, when workers begin to fix the roof, they discover that your gutters are in bad condition and you need work there. The carpenter discovers that the whole house is sagging a little, and your main beam needs to be strengthened. While he's at work in the basement, he urges you to get a plumber in to take a good look at the pipes.

The plumber explains that the old lead piping is about to go, and anyway should be replaced by copper tubing. Before you know it you've got a major renovation underway in all the pipes. You then decide that while the plumber is there you might just as well take out the old sinks and appliances and modernize the kitchen and the bathroom.

You still haven't tackled problems like the new wiring you will have to put in the house and the fact that the old heating system should be replaced. But you can see what is happening. Once you start to renovate, where do you stop?

With renewal underway, this is exactly the question religious communities are asking themselves: "Where do we stop?"

It was obvious to many people within these religious communities that some changes were necessary. Many sisters, even some older ones who loved the traditions of their founder, began to ask: "Just how important is it for us to train all of our young sisters to hold their hands just so as they enter the chapel?" Now some of the sisters, even those who wanted some change, are asking: "Shouldn't we protect ourselves from becoming so busy with the problems of the inner city that we fail to restore our own spirits with a sound prayer life?"

As most religious communities engage in this re-evaluation of their way of life, certain words appear in most conversations: "freedom," "celibacy," etc.

We have talked about the concept of community, but a basic question of today's nun is: "How much freedom should I have to do my own thing and how much should I be subject to authority?" As noted earlier, some nuns used to be rather stilted individuals—pretty much poured into the same mold. Now we see different clothes, varied hair styles, individual and unique talents emerging from religious communities. But how far can a religious community go in this direction? If a lot of individuals are "doing their thing" how can a community have cohesiveness?

Or is the emphasis wrong here? Is it true that religious orders exist not for any good to be gained for themselves, or even a church. Shouldn't dedicated Christians serve persons by sharing the gifts purchased for all people by the Crucifixion and the Resurrection?

As we mentioned, the concept of "community" is important too. Community used to mean the religious community. It now refers to the Christian or world community—all human persons. Broader outlooks are involved here. Shouldn't religious orders reach out beyond their own boundaries to the needs of the world? Shouldn't they answer social needs, not just spiritual ones? (Is there even a real distinction between social and spiritual needs?) Can women stay within the convent walls oblivious to the immorality of poverty and social injustice at a discreet distance from the convent?

Many missionaries learned long ago that it's hard to tell people God loves them if their children have no food, and if there are no medical facilities to fight disease and ease pain. Can a black high-school student really take a nun seriously in his religion class if he knows the sister has an obvious prejudice against the black community in which her convent is located?

This is the dilemma facing religious communities today. How do you "put your house in order" and modernize it?

I said I wouldn't offer solutions since I have never been a part of any religious community. However, before leaving the topic of religious life and relevancy, it will be helpful to examine the reflections of one who has lived within a religious order and has sought its renewal.

THE NEW COMMUNITY

One leading spokesmen for a new type of religious community is Brother Gabriel Moran, a member of the Christian Brothers, a congregation established to teach the poor in seventeenth-century France. Moran already had quite a reputation as a theologian when he published his first book on the religious life. The book, co-authored with a nun, Sister Maria Harris, was entitled *Experiences in Community: Should Religious Life Survive?* [30] Moran's follow-up reflections appeared two years later in a companion volume: *The New Community: Religious Life in an Era of Change.* [31]

I have selected from these two volumes some of the concepts that appear to me most significant for "new communities."

First of all, Moran feels the need for community is absolutely essential—a part of the life and death cycle of man. He adds that in the shift from small town to city we will all be destroyed unless the concept of community survives. Moran believes that if religious life were to cease, something similar to it would have to arise. However, the future of religious life depends upon utilizing the concepts of fraternity and brotherhood as models.

One of the basic challenges facing the new community, according to Moran, is to give individuals freedom to create a personal life style, and, at the same time, retain the group's identity and cohesiveness. This search for individual identity is partly the result of Freud's influence in psychology and a new movement called personalism, in which the human person emerges in twentieth-century thought. This is reflected in the new self-determination permitted within religious communities.

This dynamic drive toward freedom and personal responsibility has spread throughout society. The religious community is just one segment feeling the impact of the movement. The search for identity, says Moran, is especially necessary to the woman in religious life because she is also seeking equal treatment from the Church. (Some writers have indicated that nuns can easily identify with black individuals who want their rights because the sisters have been treated as second-class citizens also.)

Moran indicates that this identity challenge can probably best be met by having interpersonal relationships within smaller communities (perhaps six people). He says: ". . . new communities will be desperately needed that will allow for a diversity of the human while supplying a personalizing love."

Another major shift in thought is documented by Moran as he touches upon the concept of secularism. In the Church's past there has often seemed to be a conflict between the sacred and the secular—between the City of God and the City of Man. Moran says in order to change the world, the new community must accept the world as it is. This calls for social involvement with some of the revolutions of the day. (Thus, nuns in picket lines.)

This subject arises again later where we can explore some of the implications of Harvey Cox's book *The Secular City.* Here we can simply note that becoming actively involved in the world caused post-Vatican II convent walls to crumble. It meant that the specific tasks of a community (its collective apostolate) would probably have to be altered periodically, as societal changes envelop the group.

Therefore, the world of a nun will be changing from time to time. This is a sensitive area because ideally an individual's concept of his or her dignity is directly connected with the work that individual does. For new communities, this work in the world will often require secular clothing. Moran also favors freedom in religious attire.

A practical problem of new communities (like emerging nations) is the challenge of self-government. The full exercise of freedom, according to Moran, requires organization, government and leadership. Some centralized authority is essential, but the religious community, he adds, must become more democratic—especially at the local level. Structure should be minimal.

An interesting approach would be having a loose federation of communities. Perhaps some communities should be split into two parts, thus giving the members a choice of an open and free community or a more highly structured one. Many groups have already incorporated this innovation. Moran pleads for pluralism—a chance to experiment and try new ways. Thus, the great values inherent in past religious life can arise in new forms.

Most observers agree the quality of religious commitment suffers if prayer does not permeate the life style. Moran, too, agrees religious communities cannot long exist without drawing strength from a prayer life. He thinks it best if this worshipping together can be, at least to a degree, free and spontaneous.

Concerning the controversial subject of celibacy, Moran feels that a celibate group can offer a special witness to a technological world. He strongly urges, however, that this celibacy find room for the formation of enriching friendships: Many people in religious life today are desperately lonely.

Gabriel Moran has been called an impractical prophet, and his recommendations have not been accepted unanimously by all those trying to adapt religious communities to the milieu of the twentieth and twenty-first centuries. Various writers have accused Moran of being iconoclastic and one-sided in his criticism. Some have commented that he hasn't offered too many specifically practical details for working out these new communities.

Quite naturally, many of Moran's concepts are hard to evaluate because he has moved into a new context. It's hard to examine this focus properly precisely because it is all so new.

Along with prophets, religious communities need many practical leaders if they are to restructure themselves as the Vatican Council suggested and as the times seem to demand. And you can imagine how unsettling some of these changes would be to individuals who have been within religious communities for several decades and are used to a completely different context for living. This is the challenge of "the generation gap" within convents. It will call for all the patience and love dedicated religious personnel can muster to work through these renovations while still being open to one another.

As this process continues, one visible effect is the number of men and women leaving religious communities. According to a survey by the National Catholic Educational Association, the total number of nuns, priests and brothers teaching in Catholic schools declined about 12 percent within two years (1967-1969). Some individuals would remain within their religious community while moving outside of the Catholic school, but the survey indicates clearly an exodus from religious life. [32] One study shows that nuns sixty years and older now comprise 33.2 percent of the sisterhoods.

There is a challenge facing every group, whatever its apostolate or approach may be to change. Some religious will leave because changes are not being made fast enough; other nuns will decide not to stay because changes are being made too fast. Hopefully, out of the current re-evaluation process will come a life style (or a variety of them) that individuals can choose freely to enrich their lives, giving them an opportunity to be of service in a special way.

Probably in the long run it will be more important for religious communities to concentrate on *service* rather than structure. The whole purpose of such dedicated groups should be: How can we serve other persons while growing ourselves? Everything else seems to draw its importance from the concept of service—whether this is a spiritual, or a very social type of service. Sometimes "service" might even take the form of radical activism.

SCHOOLS AND OUR CHANGING SOCIETY

We have touched upon the basic financial problems forcing many Catholic schools to close their doors. And we have seen that the spiraling costs are in part the result of the increased number of lay teachers, along with major changes occurring in the structure of religious communities staffing Catholic schools. Changes such as better professional preparation carry high price tags.

Along with these very obvious changes within the Catholic schools themselves, there are dramatic alterations also in the society these schools serve.

We should, perhaps, begin with the changing character of the Catholic population in this country. Between 1940 and 1950 the population in Catholic schools doubled and everything looked hopeful for the Catholic Church. Only twenty years later we find a Church deeply troubled and conflict-ridden. What happened?

Part of the answer lies in the changing socio-economic charater of the American Roman Catholic population. When we analyze this segment of the American population we find there has been a dramatic modification in the people served by Catholic schools. This changing personality of the audience requires some adjustments in Catholic schools themselves.

The American Catholic population previously consisted primarily of immigrants, or the sons and daughters of immigrants. These people, consequently, were on the defensive, living in their ghettos in a hostile non-Catholic environment. The Catholic school was quite literally a tower of strength for these second-class citizens.

Today Catholics do just as well socially and economically as other Americans.[33] In 1970 one third of all college students in America were Catholics.

How did this rise to respectability occur?

Some say it began when Al Smith ran for President. Others point out that the GI Bill made it possible for Catholics in great numbers to obtain higher education.

Probably this "acceptance" was dramatically gained for Catholics by two men named John: John Kennedy and Pope John XXIII.

In an interesting book entitled *John F. Kennedy and American Catholicism*,[34] Lawrence H. Fuchs notes: "American heroes have been preeminently independent men of action." And "to a considerable extent John Kennedy was a symbol of the dynamic impact of the American environment on Catholicism. Like many Catholics of his generation, he esteemed not the virtues of humility, mortification, penance, chastity, poverty, . . . but those values of independence and achievement which Americans have cherished since the eighteenth century."

Kennedy was symbolic of the breed of new Catholic who was appearing, called by one writer "the generation of the third eye."[35] (The term was coined because this new group consists of a generation cut loose from many of its roots and traditions, looking constantly into itself.)

Kennedy became a cultural hero as well as America's first Catholic President. Catholics in the United States could now be more self-confident psychologically.

The other psychological lift Catholics received came from outside this country. There is no doubt that the humble and humane personality of "good Pope John" attracted the affection of non-Catholic Americans. And the Council he called showed the world that the Roman Catholic Church was trying to re-study its doctrine in the light of the needs of modern man.

The candid openness of the Vatican Council meant that the Catholic Church in America was no longer on the defensive theologically. Catholics were urged to "dialogue" with their Protestant and Jewish neighbors, visit their churches, and move into the world-wide Ecumenical Age, which, incidentally, began for the World Council of Churches as early as 1910. The military discipline and structure the Catholic Church had depended upon since the Reformation began to melt away.

This was to change the attitude of the average American Catholic and this change was bound to cause a certain amount of confusion among Catholics and non-Catholics alike.

The American Catholic Church was fast becoming a church of the suburban semi-professionals. These Catholics could no longer be counted upon to follow their parish priests unquestioningly. And this better-educated, more independent Catholic population would demand more and more of its Catholic schools. They would increasingly object to overcrowded classrooms and instruction from sisters without college degrees. They would still prefer (most of them) that their children attend a Catholic school; but they would insist that these schools prepare their sons and daughters thoroughly in secular subjects, as well as religious instruction.

Catholics were gaining self-confidence and becoming equal partners in the American dream. At the same time, however, all Americans were witnessing broad social changes in their world. These changes were so potent that someone named a disease after them— "future shock."

Alvin Toffler's best seller *Future Shock* [36] is about "what happens to people when they are overcome by change. This change overturns our institutions, shifts our values, and shrivels our roots."

The problem, according to Toffler, is that changes are occurring so rapidly and in so many areas, that we are all reeling from the blows. We don't have any systematic way to protect ourselves from this hurricane of change. Many people are not managing change; they are being chewed up by it. This led one observer to comment that the United States exhibits many qualities of an individual going through a nervous breakdown.

Change creates special problems, of course, in terms of our values. Some of these challenges are unique for Catholics, on the abortion issue, for example. However, all people—whether or not they are Catholic—face the challenge of change in their lives. Even Church leaders and theologians are challenged by change, for they must ask: "How does change affect the development of Church teaching?"

One word often used in describing society currently is alienation. Toffler describes us as a group of nomads, symbolized by Fort Lauderdale and the youthful hitchhiker who meets a variety of people, but doesn't get too involved with any of them. Adults are nomads too. In every year since 1948, one out of five Americans changed an address. Alienation flows from fragmentation of our relationships.

At the rate at which knowledge is growing, by the time today's infant is fifty years old, 97 percent of everything known in the world will have been discovered since the time that child was born. [37] Ninety percent of all the scientists who ever lived are alive right now.

With so much technology turning out so many disposable products and ideas, it's no wonder that we barely learn a fact before it's out of date. (Everything, including knowledge itself, seems to have built-in obsolescence!)

If, as Toffler claims, human beings are being tested almost beyond endurance, imagine how institutions are being buffeted about by all these changes. One such institution, of course, is the Catholic school.

When the Catholic school system was first established, and when most Catholic schools were built, the world was a very different place. These schools are still standing there trying to be of service, but the whole scene around them has changed dramatically.

Technology has revolutionized the scene, but there are other factors also. In the world of ideas, for instance.

Today we hear a great deal about rebellion—by young people, by blacks, etc. These eruptions are partly the result of changes in the world of ideas. The term "existentialism" covers one such area of changing thought.

The philosophies of existentialism and personalism are also two systems that are exploding previous modes of thought.

If present existence and the human person are most important, your whole religious frame of reference may shift from "the hereafter" to "the here and now." There is a shift from the God "out there" to God "in the midst of human experience."

Such a changing emphasis is demonstrated in one area, for example. In the past, when black people were denied their rights, they received comfort in a spiritualism promising things would be better when they "crossed over the Jordan." Many a black human being suffered, knowing that after this life was over, he would find peace. Spirituals are filled with this hope and expectancy.

Contrast this attitude with today's black rebellion: people demand equality *now.*

It may seem far-fetched to connect the current rebellion on many levels with the Existentialist writers at work in Paris during World War II, but there may be a connection. Changing ideas filter down into our everyday lives (just as the Communist Revolution was sparked in 1917 by the ideas penned by Marx half a century earlier).

These factors have created a challenge for all educational institutions. However, Catholic schools have often had the reputation of being quite rigid and inflexible. Many people are now wondering if these schools can adapt to the changing world with its far-flung freedom and its spirit of rebellion. Can Catholic schools be relevant in the "Age of Aquarius"?

Churches attempting to keep pace with change have reflected varying degrees of success or failure. The fact that many young people do not feel deep loyalty to church structures seems to indicate that organized religion may have a long way to go in speaking meaningfully to a changing world. This is definitely one area where the Catholic school must make adjustments to a changing society.

However, perhaps one role the Church should play is to be a preserver of traditions—instead of jumping on every new bandwagon. Toffler insists that in a changing world, man has an even greater need for some unchangeable things to give a feeling of stability and permanence. He says we may need to create rituals (similar to our Fourth of July celebration) to give us something to hold on to. Perhaps the churches should help maintain stability by preserving some traditions for us.

The Catholic Church surveys the current scene, re-examines her traditions and, hopefully, comes up with a synthesis that preserves the best of the past, but leads people toward an evolving future. This, in greatly simplified terms, is what is meant by "the development of doctrine" in theology.

In two specific events we can touch briefly upon the Catholic Church's evolving theology. One is quite obvious. Considered one of the outstanding religious events of this century, it is the convocation of the Ecumenical Council by Pope John XXIII. This Vatican Council was to revitalize and redirect theological investigation within the Catholic Church and outside of it. The repercussions are still being felt even a decade later, and we are unable, being so close to the event itself, to evaluate its impact properly. We do know that the Council completely altered the image of the Catholic Church in the world and changed many specific aspects of Catholicism in our country.

We shall examine later in more detail some specific applications of the Vatican Council documents to an evolving educational theory for American Catholics.

The other theological question I would like to touch upon specifically is the changing attitude toward the secular. This mini-revolution began in 1965 with the publication of a book entitled *The Secular City* by Harvey Cox, a Protestant culture hero. One Catholic writer has referred to our current "intoxication with the secular." [38]

These two areas—the Vatican Council deliberations and the debate over whether or not we really reside in "a secular city"— relate directly to the current Catholic-school dilemma.

Later we shall examine the basic Catholic philosophy of education, and contrast the papal encyclical on "The Christian Education of Youth" (issued by Pope Pius XI in 1929) with the Vatican Council's "Declaration on Christian Education" (promulgated in 1965, at the fourth session). This will help us understand the Catholic philosophy of education as we ask: "Should all Catholic schools close?"

Here, however, we can note in general, that with the deliberations of the Vatican Council, the Catholic Church undertook a general re-statement of her teachings and their significance to modern man.

This examination resulted directly in a general re-evaluation of Catholic goals and priorities. One major priority in America had been to have every Catholic child in a Catholic school. Although it had not been accomplished, millions of dollars had been invested in the effort by the American Catholic Church.

Now Catholics were asking: "Should these resources go elsewhere, since we are pouring most of our effort and funds into a system that is reaching only about half of our youth? What about our relative neglect of all the Catholic students who attend public schools?" In most parish budgets the religious education program— called the Confraternity of Christian Doctrine, or CCD—is a poor step-child because almost no funds are allocated for these CCD programs. One commentator even told me: "CCD is worse than a step-child; it's an orphan!" People began asking, "Should we invest more resources in an adult education program?"

All of this educational re-evalutaion was stirred by the basic deliberations and questions asked in Rome during Vatican II.

What about the theological disturbance created by the Harvard Divinity School professor, Harvey Cox?

In 1965, in preparation for a series of conferences by the National Student Christian Federation, Harvey Cox organized a resource booklet. He did not know at that time that his thoughts on "the secular city" would reach a much wider audience. The book became that rare combination: a theological "best seller."

Up to this time, most theologians and Church leaders felt that basically a tension existed between man's biblical faith and his life here on earth. Cox defined "secularization" as "the liberation of man . . . the turning of his attention away from other worlds and toward this one." [39]

The attitude of "involvement" was present in the early Church because these Christians did not want to abandon a world God had made and to which He would return, they believed, in visible triumph. In the Middle Ages there was no clear tension between the sanctuary and the marketplace because the Church permeated all aspects of life. The cathedral was built in the village square and life revolved around it—work, play, etc. For Cox the development of modern secular cities is not a sinister curse; it is a great opportunity. Whereas the cathedral symbolized the earlier ages, the symbols of the secular city are the switchboard (key to man's communication) and the highway cloverleaf (symbolic of man's mobility).

Cox later summed up his Christian secularity by quoting Pierre Teilhard de Chardin, the Catholic scientist-theologian-mystic-poet: "In the name of our faith, we have the right and duty to become passionate things of the earth."[40]

When dealing with the challenge of the secular, we touch upon a concept that has inspired the divergent views of Renaissance humanists and modern ecologists.

During the Renaissance there was a re-birth of learning that gave man such confidence that a special guideline was resurrected from classical Greek: "Man is the measure of all things." Man, not God, steps onto the stage as mankind's model. Centuries later, in our own age, inspired by science and technology, man again raises monuments to mankind itself—modern cities. Cox explores the theological significance of the modern metropolis—the secular city. He says it isn't all that bad. (For one thing, it offers anonymity, which Cox claims has some advantages.)

A "new image of the secular" has been presented by an eminent Jesuit, William F. Lynch in a volume entitled *Christ and Prometheus.* Father Lynch demonstrates his theory in terms of the plays of Aeschylus with their action, suffering and reconciliation. Lynch proposes that Prometheus was the great secular symbol because he first gave man fire, then the alphabet, and all the other resources by which we have been struggling out of the darkness.

This book goes beyond *The Secular City,* but is not as easily readable as Harvey Cox always is. However, Lynch feels Cox ignored the terror of the secular city. Lynch's basic premise is that "the religious imagination is in a state of serious division. It is living in a secular world but has no acceptable image of security, no image of 'the world' within which it can live and breathe."

Lynch's definition of the secular is poetic: "By secularity . . . I mean the march of mankind . . . toward the mastery and humanization of the world . . ." and he notes "the crisis is not the perennial quarrel between the religious man on the one hand and the secular man on the other. Rather, it is the struggle going on in the one man between these apparently diverse principles."

The author laments that "we have been in the midst of a great renaissance of human energy and genius. But we have also been in the midst of the terrors of our own violence . . . ." In an attempt to restore an inner unity within modern man, Lynch makes a basic theoretical and practical suggestion—we must truly reconcile Christianity and the Enlightenment, the sacred and the secular.

These ideas may seem remote from the everyday lives of most of us. However, Cox, Toffler, and Lynch are trying to explore some very basic questions facing modern man in a technological world.,

To return to our main topic, one might ask: "Should the secular city have parochial schools?" Cox does not touch upon this specific question in his book. He does, however, see a function for such private schools, but it is a role specifically tied to the needs of the modern city—such as providing an alternative educational program for black families. [41] This is a new approach to the concept of Christian witness by serving human needs.

In Part II of *The Flickering Light* we shall focus upon the question: "Should all Catholic schools close?" In other words, "Is there still a need for Catholic schools?"

So far, we have noted that the reason many Catholic schools have closed is that they have been the victim of changing faculties (to lay teachers); changing concepts of religious communities and their apostolates; changes in the society in which schools exist; the changing character of the Catholic population in America served by these schools; and changing theological concepts, including personalism and the respectability of the secular.

Like many other institutions, some Catholic schools have been chewed up by change.

PART II

Should all catholic schools close?

A recent book, analyzing American education today, opens with these words: "Ours is an age of crisis."[1]

We also know that we have a crisis in Catholic schools.

The real question is: "What should we do about it?"

Should *all* Catholic schools in America close? Is it a mistake to continue supporting a system that currently absorbs more than a billion dollars and still reaches less than 40 percent[2] of the Catholic population of school age? What about all the young Catholics who can't be accommodated within these schools? Are we neglecting the religious formation of 60 percent for the sake of 40 percent? What about all the adults we could be helping? Also, shouldn't we concentrate more on working with fellow human beings outside the Catholic Church?

Do Catholic schools meet legitimate needs anymore? Catholic schools were originally built and developed to protect Catholics from the loss of their faith in a hostile America. The immigrant who came to this country from Ireland, Germany, or Italy needed some cultural protection. He wanted a "ghetto"—to be "with his own." But now there aren't many immigrants—and their descendants have been absorbed into the American mainstream. Today's ghetto doesn't protect the Catholic—it simply separates minority groups from a white majority.

WHY DO CATHOLICS CONSIDER A SEPARATE SYSTEM?

Should the churches in America get out of the school business?

If your immediate reaction to the above question is to shout wildly "Yes!" or "No!," we aren't going to get anywhere. Too many people are shouting wildly at one another already. (One cultural historian says that the problem today is not that people lack conviction, but rather that they have too many of them.)[3]

Is your opinion based on facts? Or is it a personal, subjective strong feeling? Perhaps your viewpoint is mainly based upon an unfortunate experience with a teacher when you were a child, and this turned you against nuns. Or perhaps—at the other extreme—you are so emotionally attached to "the good sisters" you simply panic at the thought of "losing our Catholic schools."

Neither viewpoint will shed much light on this problem.

In a crisis situation the future course of action should not be determined by emotional hang-ups. For example, as the American nation has progressed on its space program, each step along the way has been researched, analyzed, and studied. This is how man walked on the moon.

Likewise, what we need—nationally, and in every diocese—is an organized appraisal of all Catholic education, including schools. Only with such a systematic study can we answer the question: "Should Catholics continue to maintain a separate school system, and, if so, should changes be made in that system?"

There are three different aspects of this problem to be explored before answering the question "Is it worth it?" We will try to investigate these areas in this section of *The Flickering Light.*

1. What are the HISTORICAL facts?
   Why *did* Catholics build these schools in the first place? What situation prompted the Catholic Church to insist upon a separate school system? Do these conditions still exist? If not, are there different, but equally compelling, reasons for the existence of a separate school system today?

2. What are the THEOLOGICAL facts?
   What philosophical and theological view of man is the basis of the Catholic educational program? Can religion be taught in public schools? In the light of the Vatican Council, what guidelines do we now have concerning the religious instruction of Catholics? Did Vatican II endorse Catholic schools? Or did the Council suggest that this approach is no longer necessary?

3. What are the SCIENTIFIC facts?
   We are just beginning to undertake serious scientific surveys of Catholic schools. What does the research indicate about the performance of Catholic schools in achieving their goals? What

do surveys show concerning the value and effectiveness of Catholic education?

Our aim is to analyze some basic facts which should lay the foundation for an informed judgment of Catholic education in America. Hopefully, this will cut down a little on all the panic and wild shouting that this sensitive topic has at times provoked.

It seems incredible, but Catholics also need to be reminded of "the facts." Some sisters staffing Catholic schools are beginning to wonder if they should serve outside of classrooms. These thoughtful questions are valid ones. However, everyone should pause long enough to reason and think things through before jumping to conclusions that are not supported by facts.

This type of thoughtful investigation should be helpful for all American parents and taxpayers. It is *vital* for dedicated Catholic educators.

WHAT ARE THE HISTORICAL FACTS?

When referring to the history of Catholic education in its broadest sense, one must begin before the actual construction of buildings. One of the earliest mandates was: "Go and teach all nations . . . ."

This type of teaching was not, of course, practiced in classrooms.

And the first type of Catholic education in America wasn't either.

The earliest educational attempts in this country were associated with the Spanish and French colonization here. Missionary priests accompanied explorers to the shores of North and South America.

The adventurers were seeking gold or furs. The missionaries sought to convert "the heathen" to Christianity. Some type of educational program was necessary to achieve this goal.

These beginnings—along with the later history of Catholic education—have been documented by educational historians Burns, Kohlbrenner and Buetow.[4]

The early segment, or colonial period, was essentially a transplantation of a European culture to American shores. And this European viewpoint was a culture permeated by the Church. Such church-state union had produced an educational effect in Europe with which most of us are familiar. The fact is—as we all learned in our history classes—the lamp of learning was kept burning during the Middle Ages by the Christian Church. In her monasteries, and later in the universities, the Church had a formal educational program that played a direct and dramatic role in the preservation of Western civilization.

The educator-historian, George N. Shuster, writes about the tradition of monasticism, and has said, very firmly ". . . the [Roman Catholic] Church will not survive without the monastic institutions."[5] Shuster repeats what we remember from our history books: "A principal source of strength has been the religious community dedicated to scholarly teaching. In the pre-Medieval world there was little Christian educational activity in any formal sense, but during the period which followed the collapse of the Roman Empire, Benedictine monasticism became a highly significant agency for keeping alive both learning and education. It was the monk, living in his abbey or answering the call of princes and bishops, who became the teacher of his time."[6]

Shuster feels that "monasticism is the ultimate source of . . . formation in the Catholic sphere." And he feels that the monastic tradition guarantees freedom. "One cannot have any kind of freedom that is to be taken seriously unless one also has some form of certainty. . . . Freedom in the Church also presupposes that one has a reasonable, personal certainty about the Church and about one's relationship with it."[7]

The cultural commentator and art historian, Kenneth Cark, also refers to monasteries as "the guardians of civilization."[8] Indeed, in such an educational structure, the study of theology, or man's relationship to God, was the core of all curriculum.

This long history of involvement with intellectual traditions must be kept in mind. We must analyze the Church's educational role in the light of her identity with learning over centuries, not just considering her American Catholic school program. For centuries the Church has been identified with the process of asking basic questions. It is this long-term relationship which is to be significantly studied. We are not just asking should some or all American Catholic school buildings close. The more important consideration is: In what way should all churches educate humanity? It's been done in monasteries; it's been done in universities; it's been done in parish schools; it's been done in "Sunday Schools." What is the best procedure now?

The American Experiment

Historically there were aspects of the American situation that were unique. Basically, the difference was to generate a new approach to the relationship of church and state.

Early English colonists after a century saw advantages in being more independent from the English crown. And even though England was not at this time a Roman Catholic nation, there still was an "established" church in England. As Americans won freedom from the king of England, it became possible for this new nation to give birth to a new church-state doctrine.

America's church-state experiment is still evolving, as we shall see when we explore the theology of Catholic education, and as we examine Supreme Court rulings in this delicate area. As a matter of fact, one of the major contributions of American thought to the recent Vatican Council was the document "Declaration on Religious Freedom." This landmark document was largely the result of the work of the American church-state theologian John Courtney Murray, S.J.[9] Thus, the church-state relationship is still a "developing doctrine." (Incidentally, some educators have tried to translate the church-state relationship into a comprehensive [public] school with an attached religious instruction center. This has been attemped in Swanton, Vermont.)

Many people are not aware that all schools in early colonial America were religious schools. Bible study and moral teachings completely permeated books and lessons from the early rural schoolroom to Harvard College—established in 1636 for the purpose of educating the "English and Indian youth in knowledge and Godliness."

In colonial America, historically, the English colonies set the standard of educational excellence. The early educational efforts of the French and Spanish were not to be lasting. Along the Atlantic seaboard, however, in English settlements, education became primarily the responsibility of the parents and the formal schools were church-controlled by existing Protestant codes.

Apparently the first formally established Catholic school in the English-speaking colonies was located at Newtowne, Maryland, about 1640. The documents seem to indicate that this school had elementary classes and college preparatory instruction as well.[10]

The foundations of the American Catholic school system were planted in the period following America's War for Independence. The man who shaped this foundation was John Carroll, a close friend of Benjamin Franklin. In 1789, Carroll became the first bishop of the Catholic Church in the United States. His personality and his background made him acceptable to Protestants in a nation not known for tolerance where its 25,000 Catholics were concerned.

As early as 1785 Carroll wrote: "The object nearest my heart now and the only one that can give consistency to our religious views in this country, is the establishment of a school, and afterwards of a seminary for young clergymen."[11]

Six years later, Carroll, in a pastoral letter, pointed out the necessity of "a pious and Catholic education of the young." He expressed the hope that young men who would be educated at the newly-founded college at Georgetown would return to their homes and become teachers in Catholic schools to be founded in their local communities.[12]

As these beginnings were taking shape, the American constitutional convention was meeting (1787), and a strong sentiment of religious liberty was expressed. There were Catholic representatives present and they shared these sentiments. Then, as now, there seemed a great desire for unity, but not uniformity. In a young nation a spirit of unity was vital. But uniformity in a country born because of a drive for independent action would appear undemocratic. This is also true today, two hundred years later.

During the colonial period (and up to about 1830), the whole mode of education in America was centered in private schools. The goals of the Protestant private schools were generally those of the Catholic schools—the preservation of religion, along with vocational preparation for a trade.

As the nation moved historically toward her own Civil War, American Catholics were affected by a series of administrative meetings held in Baltimore. Seven times between 1829 and 1884, the American Roman Catholic bishops met in council. On each occasion they wrote a Pastoral Letter to Catholics to inform them of their deliberations and legislative decrees.

Many aspects of Catholic life were dealt with, but the bishops—even this early in American history—were constantly returning to the theme of the importance of Catholic education. In a youthful American Church the development of the faith was in peril in a Protestant-oriented school. It was not simply that the schools were Protestant. The early days of American history also saw a strong anti-Catholic feeling. This obvious prejudice made life and learning difficult for Catholics who often were subjected to anti-papist tirades.

For example, in 1702, in Maryland—which had originally been a Catholic colony—special legislation was passed "to prevent the growth of popery." This law aimed at the complete destruction of Catholic education in the colony. "If any persons professing to be of the Church of Rome should keep school, or take upon themselves the education, government, or boarding of youth, at any place in the province, upon conviction such offenders should be transported to England to undergo the penalties provided."[13] However, from the "very beginning of the organized Church in the United States, education has received emphatic recognition from the various councils of the Church."[14]

In the *Appendix*, the document entitled "Historical Statements Concerning Schools for Catholics in America" indicates some of the earnest pleas of Church leaders, exhorting Catholics to support their own schools, for the protection and preservation of their Catholic faith and culture. In the *Appendix*, there is also a list of significant dates in the growth and development of education in America, with a special emphasis on Catholic-school historical highlights.

Before, during and after its Civil War, America was changing economically and educationally. Catholic education was altered by these changes. America was transformed from an agricultural to an industrial nation. This urbanization was reflected in the country's schools.

Further, there were more educational options. As the date chart (in the *Appendix*) indicates, this was an age of increasing educational opportunities. In Massachusetts, a law was passed in 1852 compelling school attendance for every child between the ages of eight and fourteen. Tax-supported free schooling became accepted. Education in public schools was greatly influenced by leaders like Horace Mann. And Charles Eliot, president of Harvard, contributed the elective system to American higher education.

During this period, the term *immigration* explains what happened to the Catholic Church and her schools. In 1821 and 1845 Ireland had potato blight and famine. When the first Baltimore Council met in 1829, there were one half million Catholics in America. When the Council convened in 1884—largely through the impact of immigration—the number of American Catholics had increased to sixteen times the earlier total to a new Catholic population figure of eight million.

Early Catholic Leadership
Early Catholic Church leaders included Archbishops such as Gibbons, Hughes, and England. Prominent lay leaders and intellectuals included two converts to the Catholic Church—Orestes Brownson and Isaac Hecker; the latter became a priest and established the Paulist order. Brownson wrote extensively, as did Hecker, who edited *The Catholic World.* Another lay person's name should be mentioned because many people feel that James A. McMaster may have been more responsible for the establishment of a separate Catholic school system than anyone else in America.[15]

The story of James McMaster recalls two aspects of our Catholic school story in America that have direct bearing on today's controversy.

First of all, almost every factor brought into discussion today was part of the controversy then. To have a Catholic school or not to have one was fiercely debated among Catholics themselves between 1870 and 1900. Thus, the pros and cons are not unique to our own quite sophisticated discussions.

The other interesting thing is that in the nineteenth century, it was a lay person, McMaster, who sparked the drive for separate schools, not the clergy or the bishops. And a current commentator (a layman), has once again accused Catholic educators—sisters, priests, and bishops—of a lack of dynamic leadership.[16]

History, thus, confirms this basic ingredient in the Catholic school story: the Catholic schools in America belong to the people themselves. The Catholic laity wanted them, they built them, and, if they want them to continue, lay people will have to work hard to support them.

James McMaster was such an indefatigable worker. He "has no equal in his influence on the religious and theological development of American Catholicism."[17]

McMaster was a competent writer who edited the influential New

York *Freeman's Journal* between 1847 and 1886. As with Brownson, who was also a writer, a pen places a powerful tool in the hands of such a layman.

For years, here in America, and through his contacts in Rome, McMaster pushed in his writings for parochial schools. The result was the document, confirmed by Pope Pius IX, known as the "Instruction of 1875." This "Instruction" urged bishops and people to erect their own schools to protect the faith of American Catholics. This policy "seems to have been brought about by the laity, and . . . the rigorists were the laity and the moderates were the archbishops and bishops of the country. The whiplash was in the hands of a convert lay educator."[18]

While reviewing this American history, it may be wise to stop for a few moments to consider some ideas that were European, but made their way to America and influenced her political system and her educational outlook.

"The Enlightenment" is a term applied to the main trend of thought in eighteenth-century Europe. The champions of the Enlightenment sought to popularize a rational and scientific approach to religious, social, political and economic issues.Freedom, reason, and humanitarianism were the common mottoes. Popularization was the preferred weapon. Our government is a child of eighteenth-century rationalism.

Enlightenment writers in Europe greatly affected men like Thomas Jefferson. In spirit, the Declaration of Independence reflects his debt to English Enlightenment political theorists, particularly John Locke, and to French and other continental philosophies.

Even today—two centuries later—revolutionary fires are being ignited by the concepts of the universal brotherhood of man and government "of the people." But all of these noble ideas could not be achieved without broadening the educational base. The minds of youths and adults had to be trained, if the world was to depend upon man's reason, as the Enlightenment writers suggested.

John Courtney Murray indicated, however, that the Enlightenment can't take all the credit for our independence. "The American Bill of Rights is not a piece of eighteenth-century rationalist theory; it is far more the product of Christian history. Behind it one can see, not the philosophy of the Enlightenment, but the older philosophy that had been the matrix of the common law. The 'man' whose rights are guaranteed in the face of law and government is, whether he knows it or not, the Christian man, who had learned to know his own personal dignity in the school of Christian faith."[19]

Catholic schools in America, however, were struggling in a largely anti-Catholic country, and the philosophical ideals of the Enlightenment made few inroads in a school system living in a state of siege.

As America approached and moved into the twentieth century, the nation was to become involved in a major war—World War I. The educational world was still reeling from the publication of Darwin's *Origin of Species* (in 1859), and the term evolution frightened both Catholics and fundamentalist Protestants. The whole question of the Bible's validity was challenged because of the apparently contradictory narrative of man's creation.

New influences in American education included John Dewey's ideas, upon which the structure of progressive education was to be built. In 1914, with the establishment of Teacher's College at Columbia University, a vehicle was created through which Dewey's ideas could spread out into American classrooms.

Between the years 1918 and 1957 Catholic education matured. These years can now be considered the "adolescent phase" of the system. For in many ways what happened here is similar to the growth spurt of a teenager, and the questioning and doubt accompanying such growth.

Spanning two centuries Americans have surveyed a variety of experiences: Pearl Harbor; Hitler and World War II; nativism and the Ku Klux Klan; the invention of the automobile; and the Red scare. Buetow also says the 1940s were dominated by Ernest Hemingway and the 1950s can be called "the appliance age."[20]

Most significant for its impact on American education was the year 1957. In October of that year Americans were stunned by the launching of the world's first satellite, the Russian Sputnik I. As a result, American education began a painful self-analysis. Such self-analysis leads to the height of adult maturity; it is also, however, quite characteristic of adolescents lacking self-confidence. American educators and the general public wanted to know why Russia could accomplish this dramatic space feat. What was the matter with our own educational system? Why were we apparently so far behind in the scientific field?

Educational Criticism

While public school educators examined their consciences, John Tracy Ellis was challenging American Catholic intellectual maturity. Monsignor Ellis claimed that American Catholics "have suffered from the timidity that characterizes minority groups, from the effects of a ghetto they have themselves fostered, and, too, from a sense of inferiority induced by their consciousness of the inadequacy of Catholic scholarship."[21]

Ellis added: "The chief blame, I firmly believe, lies with the Catholics themselves. It lies in their frequently self-imposed ghetto mentality which prevents them from mingling as they should with their non-Catholic colleagues, and in their lack of industry . . . ."[22]

This situation was complicated by a tragic irony. ". . . To whom, one may ask, may the leaders of the coming generations turn with more rightful

53

expectancy in their search for enlightenment and guidance in the realm of religion and morality than to the American Catholic intellectuals? For it is they who are in possession of the oldest, wisest, and most sublime tradition of learning that the world has ever known."[23] (Of course, many modern youth would also remind us that similar traditions have existed in the East.)

Therefore, faced with the challenge of Ellis, American Catholic education entered a new decade. And the 1960s elevated educational soul-searching to the level of a fine art.

On the one hand, in Catholic education, parents made unprecedented demands, forcing a growth that was to peak, as we've seen, in the middle of the sixties. (These demands, for example, have resulted in a respectable pupil-teacher ratio in Catholic schools. In 1970-71 it was 30.5 to 1 at the elementary level, and 20.8 to 1 in Catholic high schools.) On the other hand, serious questions were asked concerning Catholic education in light of the Vatican Council. The one asking sensitive questions was not a priest-professor, like Monsignor Ellis, but a woman—a Catholic parent who asked boldly: *Are Parochial Schools the Answer?*[24]

At first, the self-examination was a healthy, positive re-evaluation of Catholic educational goals. This was required in the light of the new directions indicated by the Vatican Council. In many instances, however, this potentially helpful reappraisal turned into panic and despair. This is exactly why we began this historical analysis by comparing the current Catholic-school crisis to the one outlined in the public-school study *Crisis in the Classroom.* The problems analyzed in this Carnegie Report on Education are not exclusively public school problems. Catholic schools must face the same challenges. And Catholic educators should take heart from the knowledge that many of their current difficulties are not confined to Catholic schools alone. Public-school colleagues are "crisis-ridden" too.

The Carnegie Corporation of New York funded a three-and-a-half-year study of public education, under the direction of noted journalist-scholar Charles E. Silberman. The study's report, *Crisis in the Classroom,* calls for a remaking of American education. Many Catholic leaders have demanded something just as radical to give Catholic education the dramatic new thrust demanded by the Vatican Council and by our changing times.

Neither public schools nor Catholic schools can be saved by a little first aid and few bandages. Major surgery is required, according to Silberman's diagnosis.

Silberman's chief complaint about public schools is repeated often throughout the book: What is most wrong with American education is its failure to develop sensitive, autonomous, thinking, humane individuals.

"Our most pressing educational problem, in short, is not how to increase the efficiency of the schools; it is how to create and maintain a humane society." This is almost exactly what has prompted a post-Vatican II examination of conscience in Catholic schools. Most Catholic educators have felt that their own unrest and dissatisfaction seemed unique. It isn't. Soul searching is underway in public education also.

Recent studies have shown that Catholic schools perform well in passing on to students the basic academic material, as well as factual religious information. However, student graduates are not so outstanding in the area of ethical attitudes. This causes grave concern among Catholics who feel that the Church's educational program must produce socially aware citizens to justify the Church's investment in a vast educational system. The product of a Catholic education, some note, should be the moral man: a humane decision-maker. Here we see that the creation of a humane society is a task that both public and private schools are aiming for, but not achieving, at the present time.

Silberman notes that the challenge of achieving social awareness becomes very specific when dealing with the educational needs of the inner-city poor. Here again we find a problem that currently plagues Catholic schools, but is not unique to them.

Silberman is the author of a previous work on the American race problem. He shows great sensitivity in his analysis of education and equality. He outlines specific solutions, Chicago's CAM Academy, for example. The school, sponsored by a consortium of eight Protestant and Catholic churches, is located in a decaying neighborhood that turned from all white to all black in the early 1960s. Here, clearly, is a model for Catholic educators to study if they want to be humane witnesses.

Other specific models held up by Silberman include: the informal education approach of the new primary schools in England; flexible modular scheduling; employment of the new technology, such as instructional television; and curriculum reform in physics and other areas. All these innovations have worked their way into Catholic schools, to varying degrees. And one could add others to Silberman's list: Montessori methods, open campus schools, etc.

Silberman liberally sprinkles his educational analysis with the words of John Dewey, and it is amazing how many of these quotations sound like the introduction to a Catholic school's student handbook. For example, from Dewey's *Moral Principles in Education*: "The moral purpose is universal and dominant in all instruction."[25]

All schools are currently caught up in "the revolution of rising expectations," according to Silberman. In Catholic schools this is the direct result of the Vatican Council deliberations, and the current attempts by all churches to serve all people in meaningful ways.

Can schools—either public or private—meet these challenges? One educational reformer lamented that it's easier to put a man on the moon than to reform the schools.

Thus, after two hundred years of Catholic educational activity in America, the Catholic school system seems to be undergoing an identity crisis of its own. In fact, though, public schools are suffering through a parallel crisis, right along with Catholic schools.

WHAT ARE THE THEOLOGICAL FACTS?

The Dean of the Harvard Divinity School perceptively commented: "Religion and education have been married, divorced, and re-married so often in their long history that it is easy to say that they cannot get along with each other any better than they can do without each other."[26]

This statement was made by Samuel Miller as he participated in a Conference on the Role of Religion in Public Education, held at Harvard University in 1966. The Conference brought together leading Catholic, Protestant, and Jewish minds to grapple with the basic problems summarized by Dean Miller:

1. In a democracy, you are committed to respect different viewpoints. How, then, do you handle the topic of religion in the public-school classroom?
2. Should public schools even get involved in the topic of religion? Is it possible to treat such a touchy subject objectively?
3. On the other hand, is it unfair to our youth to deprive them of an awareness of religious concepts and values? Do public schools have a responsibility to train moral, religiously-aware citizens?
4. How is it possible to agree on which morality or religion is the right one without offending the rights of the other students who have different beliefs, or no beliefs?

This dilemma forms the basis of the establishment of a separate school system by the Roman Catholic Church in America. Catholics in this country have been fully aware of the difficulties of inculcating specific religious values in public-school classrooms. This has been the prime factor behind the establishment of these private schools.

The Catholic theology of education is based, ultimately, upon a special view of man. The basis for this viewpoint is that man has a unique nature—a body and a soul. Modern personalism stresses the cooperation between body and soul, rather than the tension existing between them.

However, this theology notes that it is on the intellectual and spiritual level that man is unique. Other animals also have bodily needs. But man has the opportunity to enjoy sensual pleasures, along with the desire for sublime intellectual and spiritual heights.

Therefore, the Catholic philosophy or theology of education notes that to be concerned only about a youth's grade in modern math, or a college student's physics score, is entirely too limited. These students must learn math, and it is the specific purpose of any school to train minds. But, the formation of the people of God on pilgrimage is the broad goal of all Catholic educational programs. Of course, the formation occurs within individual persons, not within groups collectively.

It might be wise to consider, too, the distinction between education and schooling. The term education is a broad one. We are educated in many ways that have nothing whatsoever to do with schools. Marriage provides an educational experience; television programming at times educates; a person can be educated by a personal tragedy, or a trip to Europe. The term schooling or training, however, refers specifically to formal instruction—usually given in a structured school setting.

Now, it's perfectly clear that a Catholic educational program need not be tied exclusively to schools. Many experiences can be provided by churches to accomplish a teaching goal: a good sermon; the moral example of her leaders; newspapers. The liturgy or worship, itself, is instructional.

What is basic, in terms of maturation, is this: as a child develops physically, emotionally, and psychologically, Catholic educators would have him mature spiritually as well.

Classical, Medieval and Enlightenment Foundations of Thought

A broad view of man was influenced greatly by the early philosophical writings of the Greeks Plato and Aristotle. Aristotle rejected the Platonic view of the world, but some of the key concepts of both men have been incorporated into contemporary American thought. Don't these early classical ideas sound familiar?

1. There is a regularity in the processes of nature, so this must reflect an intelligent mind behind it (an eternal prime mover).
2. In ethics, as in politics, the most important thing is what is good for man's happiness.
3. The psyche (or soul) is the source of motion for man and for the whole world.

During the sixth century, the Roman philosopher Boethius wanted to show the profound harmony between Plato and Aristotle, so he set about translating their writings into Latin. And this achievement helped make possible the transmission of Greek philosophical thought and Aristotelian logic to Latin Christendom.

During the Middle Ages, Catholic thinkers (especially Thomas Aquinas, who lived from 1225-1274) rediscovered the genius of Aristotle, and built a philosophical system upon his foundation. With these Greek intellectual tools, the Christians hammered out a rigorous system of thought. This view of man and his world is articulated in "scholastic philosophy." This system of thought, therefore, represents a synthesis, or combination, of faith and reason. Six centuries later it was given impetus by Pope Leo XIII, particularly through his encyclical "Aeterni Patris" in 1879.

The Renaissance contributed its view of man when its writers quoted Protagoras: "Man is the measure of all things." Here we see reinforced the basic Greek concept of the value of the individual. Now man is the focal point to which all other things converge.

In later centuries, specifically the seventeenth and eighteenth, science and Enlightenment developed as a part of our flowering bud of philosophy. Whereas theology (the study of revealed religious thought) had reigned as the most noble study at medieval universities, the intellectual man now worshipped at the altar of science and reason. The scientific method ruled inquiry now, and if a proposition couldn't be demonstrated in a laboratory, it was doubted.

Actually this movement from religious orthodoxy to anti-religious reaction usually spans two centuries. In Europe, the seventeenth century was a time of individual scientific discoveries by basically orthodox Christians who did not use the discoveries to attack religion. In the eighteenth century, came an anti-clerical, anti-religious reaction, built upon the science of the preceding century. In America, the anti-religious reaction occurred in the nineteenth century; in Russia, the anti-religious reaction occurred (after Tolstoy and Gogol) in the twentieth century.

The strongest conviction of the Enlightenment, actually, was that right reasoning could find true knowledge and would lead, ultimately, to man's happiness. Of great importance was intellectual freedom, but freedom was not enough. Correct reasoning would require better education.

Many observers have noted that the secularization of American society was underway by the time of the American Revolution, and the liberal philosophers of the Enlightenment must accept the praise or the blame for this. The fact is that experience had seriously challenged tradition, and individualism challenged authority. We are, even today, living out the results of this dramatic change. These concepts, defended vigorously now, found roots here: all men are linked by nature in a universal brotherhoood; war is the great enemy of civilization; government is derived from the consent of the governed; and there is an ultimate right of rebellion.

"We hold these truths . . ." is a key phrase used by Jefferson and the Founding Fathers in our Declaration of Independence. And it is the title of a book written by the American churchman who, more than anyone else, synthesized the twin ideals of religious liberty and man's search for truth.

The Jesuit, John Courtney Murray, wrote *We Hold These Truths* in 1960.[27] He was, as already mentioned, to become one of the chief architects of the Vatican Council's "Declaration on Religious Freedom."

Other sciences were also affecting this developing view of man, especially in connection with how we handle the child in the classroom. The two basic influential thinkers were Jean Jacques Rousseau, and Sigmund Freud.

Rousseau, the author of the work *Emile*, stressed that man was naturally good. Actually, he felt that man was born neither good nor bad, but with certain potentialities which he strives to realize. *Emile* designed a plan for education to make an ordinary, "natural" child morally and intellectually rational. These basic ideas of the eighteenth century were critically evaluated by Pope Leo XIII, and were to reappear in the twentieth in the progressive education of John Dewey and his followers.

Today's schools of education are heavily laden with various psychology courses. The hidden aspects of man's psyche were explored centuries ago by the Greeks. The modern psychological pioneer was Sigmund Freud. All education has been affected by psychoanalysis, which he began single-handedly.

It is probably true, however, that Catholic education in America has been so busy erecting structures and simply getting itself built, that most of its classrooms were not directly affected by Freudian analysis, and would have been shocked by such a suggestion. (As a matter of fact, the bold assertions by Freud that most of man's actions were affected by his sexual drive made most Catholic educators uneasy.) It does remain true, however, that a philosophy, or view of man, must today have a psychological dimension.

In our search for an understanding of man and a philosophy of education, we first traveled back to Aristotle's Athens, and concluded our trip in Freud's Vienna. You may be tempted to ask: "Was this trip necessary?"

It may seem irrelevant to speak of "a philosophy or theology of education," so to put the concept in a more practical context, we can simply ask: "What is the *purpose* of a Catholic school?"

It was interesting to see Charles Silberman tackle the parallel question for the public schools in his educational best-seller, *Crisis in the Classroom*. Silberman notes that Conant and many other educators express boredom when someone wants them to discuss the purpose of schools.[28]

In spite of Conant's reputation (or, perhaps, because of it), Silberman adds curtly: "But philosophical questions neither disappear nor resolve themselves by being ignored."

For Catholics, the question of the purpose of Catholic education is a crucial one for, ultimately, this will help determine whether the Church should maintain a school system, or attempt new educational approaches.

At the earlier-mentioned Harvard Conference on the Role of Religion in Public Education, in 1966, the Jesuit educator, Neil McCluskey, briefly stated the religious and educational justification for a Catholic school. "Catholics generally agree that the objectives of religious education are ideally realized in an atmosphere wherein the spiritual and the supernatural are properly ordered in a hierarchy of values."[29a] The Catholic educational goal, therefore, would be the mature, thinking human being. More specifically even, for Catholics, it would be developing the capacity to respond by commitment in faith to Christ. The systematic study of religious doctrine is better achieved in a separate, religiously oriented school, for a person learns religion in somewhat the same way that he learns a language. If he is fortunate enough to be raised in the country where the tongue is spoken, he will almost always have a better grasp of the language than he would have through intense self-instruction or private tutoring or enrollment in a special class. The atmosphere of a religiously oriented school definitely reinforces and hastens the learning process. Above all, in a thousand subtle ways that defy definition, this atmosphere strengthens and completes the educational influence of home and church, No one has perfectly analyzed or described it. Exaggerated claims have been made for it. Hostile critics have labeled it brainwashing. And perhaps it is a form of conditioning—but in the same respectable category with the process that results in love of country or family."[29b]

McCluskey obviously feels such a school has a unique value, even today. However, he adds: "A separate parochial school in America as a system to provide for the total schooling of Catholic children was born of desperate necessity. It might never have come about—at least on the scale it did—had the mood of nineteenth century America been different." And he concludes: "The separate religiously oriented school will continue to play a key role for a significant portion of the school population, . . . perhaps at no time in history has America had greater need for a distinctive witness of this type of school."

Christian Education of Youth

There are two basic "official" documents on the subject of Christian education. The first is the Encyclical Letter on *Christian Education of Youth*, issued in 1929 by Pope Pius XI.

This statement must be studied in the context of its times. And readers who are not Catholic will realize that this is the Roman Catholic Church's official authority speaking to Catholics. Believers probably would view Christian education this way (just as the Amish have their own view of dangers of public school education). It seems only democratic to respect these various views and the rights all individuals have to hold such views. This position has recently been strengthened by the Supreme Court in the Amish case. This decision, of significance on several different levels, was announced by the United States Supreme Court in May, 1972. In this landmark religious liberty decision, the Court ruled that forcing Amish parents to send their children to high school violates the parents' constitutionally-protected right to practice their religion. It was a nearly-unanimous ruling. The court strongly held that secondary schooling could expose Amish children to values contrary to their beliefs and ways of life. This case clearly offers future guidelines in the profoundly significant areas of parental rights, the public good, and religious freedom.

In 1929, the Pope defended the basic right of parents and the Church, along with the state, to determine a child's formation. One has only to reflect on the alternative in its worst form: the dictatorial and evil control over youth that marked Hitler's grasp of power in the years immediately following this papal appeal.

It may seem over-dramatic to re-emphasize parental rights today. We have seen some advantages to the kibbutz, as well as to the hippie commune life-style. Yet, such a restatement can be helpful when you consider that if there is no alternative school system in America—if there is, in effect, no choice on the part of parents between a public school and something else—then American parents have, in effect, lost the authority over their child's education. If there is only one school system, you have created a subtle educational dictatorship. The right of parents to choose is simply a moot question.

Here are a few of the main principles stressed by Pope Pius XI in his encyclical letter.

Education is of the utmost importance because it bears directly on the most important and crucial aspect of man's existence—the purpose or final goal of his life.

Education is a social activity, not an individual one. And man is born into three societies—the family, the state, and the Church. Consequently, education is the concern of all three groups in society.

The Church has a right to an active role in education because of the mandate of the Church's founder: "Go and teach all nations." And if she is a true supernatural mother, then she has a right and an obligation to supervise the educational development of all her children in everything that concerns religion and morality.

The Pope also insisted that children do not belong to the state, but to the family. Therefore, the family has the prior educational right. The state, however, does have the right and the obligation to promote the education of youth in various ways, in order to form good citizens. However, the state must respect the rights and duties of parents and of the Church in the educational process.

While education should not be despotic or dictatorial, educators must remember that human nature has been weakened by original sin, counseled the Pope, and total educational emancipation could bring educational chaos.

The most famous quotation from this encyclical is: ". . . the true Christian, product of Christian education, is the supernatural man who thinks, judges and acts constantly and consistently in accordance with right reason illumined by the supernatural light of the example and teaching of Christ; in other words, to use the current term, the true and finished man of character."[30]

The Declaration on Christian Education

It is interesting to compare (and contrast) the second official educational document with the first. On October 28, 1965, Pope Paul VI released the Second Vatican Council's *Declaration on Christian Education.*[31]

What did this statement conclude about Catholic schools? First of all, it repeated that the Church must be concerned with the whole of man's life. Therefore, the Church has a role in the progress and development of education.

The Council insisted that "all people of every race, condition and age, since they enjoy the dignity of a human being, have an inalienable right to an education that is in keeping with this ultimate goal, their ability, their sex, and the culture and tradition of their country . . . ."

Psychological advances are to be used in education, according to the Council statement, which also encourages "a positive and prudent sexual education."

Vatican II reinforced the concept that the right to education of the child is shared by the state, the Church, and the child's parents. This means that parents must have freedom of choice. "Consequently, the public power, which has the obligation to protect and defend the rights of citizens, must see to it, in its concern for distributive justice, that public subsidies are paid out in such a way that parents are truly free to choose, according to their conscience the schools they want for their children."

Repeating the importance of a Christian education, the document refers to the ". . . most serious obligation to see to it that all the faithful, but especially the youth who are the hope of the Church, enjoy [a] Christian education."

This Christian education should be in a school, if possible, according to the Council statement. "Among all educational instruments the school has a special importance. It is designed not only to develop with special care the intellectual faculties but also to form the ability to judge rightly, to hand on the cultural legacy of previous generations, to foster a sense of values, to prepare for professional life."

The Council recognizes that today's school will take on a new look in many places. ". . . The Catholic school is to take on different forms in keeping with local circumstances. Thus the Church [greatly admires] those Catholic schools, found especially in the areas of the new churches, which are attended also by students who are not Catholics." Other types of schools are encouraged, such as professional and technical schools, centers for educating adults and promoting social welfare, schools for the retarded, and schools for preparing teachers for religious instruction.

To summarize, the Catholics have built a separate school system in America quite simply because they have felt that a child's education should not be deprived of continuing consideration of man's encounter with the divine. In America, historically, Catholics were pushed to the position of separate schools when they were prevented from carrying on the task of religious formation in schools that were "public" and, for the most part, historically Protestant. This Catholic educational system often offered discipline, calm, the personal approach of a small school, in addition to religiously committed and dedicated teachers.

Many Catholic educators have agreed that it probably would have been better if such a separate school system had not been necessary. But, historically, it appeared to be necessary.

Certainly things are different now. Or are they?

It surely is true that the Catholic Church is no longer a ghetto group of immigrants. Catholics have moved into the middle and upper classes, have achieved professional status, and one of them has even resided in the White House. In an Ecumenical Age many old antagonisms are slowly decreasing, if not disappearing altogether. However, some analysts have indicated that there are still compelling reasons for Catholic schools. Along with Neil McCluskey's statement of purpose for such schools, referred to earlier, other factors have been cited.

Since the Supreme Court decision declaring it unconstitutional to have prayers in public schools, it is more obvious than ever that religious practices and formation will not be permitted within the nation's public-school system. Where do parents turn who want this religious-education formation within a school setting for their children? (Not, of course, that prayer in a classroom alone constitutes a religious milieu. However, the high court's decision is somewhat symbolic of a trend toward secularity within America's public school system.)

Other commentators insist that Catholic schools should not desert the urban poor who, now especially, need special options. For years "the poor" meant immigrant Catholics who were protected, while they were educated, by their schools. Today, living in many of the same sections of our urban areas where the immigrant used to dwell, are blacks and Spanish-speaking residents. Should the Catholic Church, after gallantly serving earlier generations, now close the very schools that would offer alternative educational choices in today's poverty pockets? Reflecting a truly Christian concern for the urban poor, many diocesan school systems are naming some of these schools "priority schools."

One compelling reason for continuing Catholic schools is the argument that there must not be a monopoly in education; this would certainly be the case if there were no schools except public schools.

These, and other considerations will be explored further after we have studied the scientific facts. We should now turn from the question "Why build separate schools?" to the other question: "How well have Catholic schools performed in the past?" In other words, have Catholics achieved their instructional goals with a separate school system in America?

WHAT ARE THE SCIENTIFIC FACTS?

Catholic schools have discovered statistics and sociology.

It's hard to believe that Catholic schools existed for about three hundred years in America before significant scientific studies were attempted concerning their effectiveness.[32] However, it wasn't until the publication of *The Education of Catholic Americans* by Andrew Greeley and Peter Rossi, in 1966, that any such extensive study was available. About the same time, another research study appeared, entitled *Catholic Schools in Action*. This survey was conducted at Notre Dame.

Many other institutions have operated for hundreds of years without gathering significant scientific data on their programs. The science of statistical analysis has become a highly-developed skill only recently.

But imagine that you are a Proctor and Gamble executive. Can you conceive of spending millions of dollars on promoting a product without conducting research? You'd want to gather data on these important questions:

What kind of product does the public need and want?
What suggestions can the consumer give on his wishes on the product?
What is the best way to "sell" this product?
Does the product really do the job we claim it does?
If the product is out-of-date, how can we modernize it?

Some may argue that the Church is a mystery, a paradox—not a corporation. It is true that a religious mission is not the same as selling soap. Yet, the efficiency of that mission will be improved by borrowing some scientific analysis techniques.

Until the publication of the Greeley-Rossi report we had almost no scientific facts on such topics related to Catholic schools. Now we do have some research on the question of just how effective Catholic schools are. This is only the beginning. We must continue to evaluate Catholic education scientifically. The more facts we gather, the better equipped we will be to make plans for the future, and to improve our product constantly.

An appropriate lesson lies in the field of medical research. Exciting announcements are made daily about advancements in medicine. Why? Because, in laboratories all over the world, research is undertaken constantly. This experimentation is giving us the ever more exciting headlines about artificial hearts, organ transplants, and cures for various cancers. Without constant scientific analysis these advances would be impossible.

Likewise, an ongoing program of experimentation and evaluation is vital to the effectiveness of Catholic education.

In fact, a national office where such constant evaluation is administered for the good of all Catholic educational programs offers tremendous educational value. In 1969, the National Catholic Educational Association received a Carnegie Foundation grant to establish such expanded research activities. NCEA studied the feasibility of a national Data Bank for Catholic education. This research Data Bank now collects, stores, and disseminates information on Catholic educational efforts throughout America through a standardized data-collection procedure. Dr. George Elford, NCEA Research Director, assured me in a recent conversation that this Data Bank is now institutionalized. The data of statisticians and sociologists should be coordinated in this way. Thus, all educational programs, public and private, national and international, can have access to the results.

In this process, many new and imaginative programs can be evaluated. After investigation, some would be discarded; others would be altered and improved; and the best could become common in schools quickly. However, all these cases presuppose organized and effective scientific research on Catholic education to guide us if we hope to develop creative educational programs.

We must beware, though, of constantly postponing action while more and more studies are conducted. William E. Brown issued this warning a few years after the Greeley-Rossi study appeared.[33]

One way to answer the question "What are the scientific facts concerning Catholic school performance?", is to take a serious look at the Greeley-Rossi report. If research and statistical tables don't scare you, study the entire document. It's available in hard-cover and paperback editions.[34]

Even some Catholic-school personnel, however, have told me that they get a headache wading through statistical charts, so we'll attempt a capsule summary.

The Greeley-Rossi study tried to find answers to certain questions about how Catholic school students and graduates compare with Catholic children who attended public schools. To summarize the report, I shall list each of the key questions explored by the Greeley-Rossi research. Then I'll explain the answers found.

Such a short summary of the data avoids headaches. The statements may appear to be sweeping generalizations, but the scientific facts supporting each statement are reported completely in the pages of the Greeley-Rossi study. Page references are noted (from the hard-cover edition), so you can study the analysis of each topic at length if you wish to probe more deeply into the scientific data.

Are Catholic-school students, or graduates, better Catholics than those who went to public schools?

It is very difficult to point to two people and say "this person is a better Catholic than that person." The researchers presumed that the "better" Catholic would probably go to Mass, Confession, and Communion more frequently. He would be more inclined to acknowledge the right of the Church to teach, and he would probably reflect the Church's "official" stand on controversial matters. He would have a more accurate knowledge of the formal teachings of the Catholic Church. He would tend to be more charitable and loving to others.

The Greeley-Rossi research DID show that Catholic school students or graduates tend to be better Catholics. People who have been to Catholic schools are more apt to do all of the above mentioned things, things that you would tend to identify with a "better" Catholic.

In the vocabulary of the social scientist: "There were statistically significant differences" between the Catholic who had been to a Catholic school and the Catholic who had been to a public school. (p. 55)

The problem is that there isn't a *dramatic* difference between them. The research showed clearly that Catholic schools do have an effect on producing better Catholics. But if the Catholic schools don't have a dramatically significant effect, we are still left with the question: "Is it worth so much effort and money to produce Catholics who are only somewhat better?"

Is the Catholic-school student more apt to get involved in Church activities later?

The Greeley-Rossi survey showed that Catholics who had attended Catholic elementary and secondary schools were more likely than others to belong to church organizations later and to be active in them. They are more likely to contribute more than $200 per year to the support of their parish. They are more inclined to discuss things seriously with a clergyman and to have a member of the clergy visit their homes.

However, again we have a problem. The researchers admitted that there isn't a particularly strong relationship between the Catholic schooling and these church activities: they added that "It must be confessed that the failure of the Catholic-school Catholics to be more tightly integrated into the Catholic community than they are is somewhat surprising." (p. 71)

It appears that many American Catholics have been active in their church organizations, but this activity is only moderately affected by the kind of education the Catholic has received.

Are Catholic schools divisive? Do they lead Catholics to non-involvement in community activities?

There is no doubt that one of the most serious criticisms leveled at Catholic schools in the past, and continuing right up to the present, comes from the feeling that it is somehow "un-American" to divide students into public-school children and private-school children. Many Americans feel that it would be in the best interest of our nation to have one unified public school system serving all American children, regardless of race, creed, or color. This cry for one system has arisen again with the discussion of a voucher plan for financing schools. The voucher approach (to be analyzed in Part III of *The Flickering Light*) would definitely provide financial support for many varieties of schools and educational systems.

This question of divisiveness is a very sensitive topic for most people, so it is especially important to have facts when considering it. Emotions get involved here on both sides. Catholics feel emotional in favor of their schools; and many other people honestly feel Catholics (and voucher advocates) are weakening the strength and solidity of the American public-school system, and, thus, contributing to the polarization of American society. Such fundamental questions are too important to be determined by emotional responses.

In studying whether Catholic schools are divisive, the social scientists tried to determine:

- • • whether Catholic-school Catholics are less likely to have Protestants and Jews as friends, neighbors, or co-workers;
- • • whether they are less inclined to engage in community activities (for example, the United Fund, PTA groups, Boy Scouts, or League of Women Voters),
- • • whether they are less well informed on secular topics, like current events.

Naturally, while youth are enrolled in a Catholic school, most of their friends and activities would involve other Catholic-school children with whom they study and play. However, the Greeley-Rossi report showed NO divisive influence later. Catholic-school Catholics are just as likely as public-school Catholics to be interested in community affairs and to have Protestant and Jewish visitors, friends, neighbors, and co-workers. (p. 236) When given a brief general-knowledge test, Catholic-school Catholics scored significantly higher than others. Thus, Catholic students are apparently more concerned about current events than those attending public schools. (p. 120) (One commentator recently told me: "Catholic schools *should* produce revolutionaries!" Certainly concerned human beings should be the result of a religious educational formation. In this sense, Catholic-school graduates should perhaps be somewhat divisive.)

Are Catholics who attended Catholic schools more rigid and intolerant in their attitudes?

The social scientists analyzing the "tolerance" of Catholic-school graduates came up with a clear-cut indication that the Catholic-school graduate is just as socially aware as the Catholic who attended public school. (p. 123) "Catholic-school Catholics are actually more tolerant with regard to civil liberties and are no more anti-Negro, anti-Semitic, or anti-Protestant. Neither are there any differences . . . in religious extremism, and permissiveness. While there is no evidence of divisive attitudes among the Catholic educated, neither is there any evidence (except in the matter of civil liberties) of more social consciousness." (p. 137)

So, once again, we have a mixed blessing. Certainly this shows that Catholic schools are not forming graduates with unreasonable prejudices against racial and religious groups. However, in order to justify the huge expense of a Catholic-school system, shouldn't Catholic schools produce Catholics with a positive sense of social justice and awareness? This is asking a great deal of any institution, but it would seem to be a fair return for the Church's investment in her vast educational program. The Catholic-school graduate—if his education has really meant something—should have a much more enlightened and open attitude toward all people, regardless of race, color, or creed. (By social awareness here, we mean sensitivity to the needs of society, for example, the educational and medical needs of the poor, equality in housing and employment. We do *not* refer to social needs based on a mere materialistic race for goods and products.)

Perhaps one reason Catholic schools produced only slightly more socially aware Catholics has been the fact that church schools have, in the past, emphasized sexual morality. Much more attention has probably been given to the moral dilemma of birth control than to the moral evil of race prejudice or war. Our entire American culture, as a whole, has been guilty of this imbalance of emphasis, not just the Catholic Church. Social awareness is developing in our culture, and this trend will certainly have an effect on both public and private school students in the future. These future students should show that Catholic schools have moved along with this trend (and, hopefully, even given the trend leadership).

Incidentally, an earlier in-depth study on one parochial school *did* indicate a broad awareness of social problems among the Catholic-school students there. Joseph H. Fichter, in the 1958 volume *Parochial School: A Sociological Study*, said: "The pupils of St. Luke's School demonstrated more favorable attitudes than the public-school children on practically all of the statements made concerning concrete social problems of the adult world." Fichter concluded: "There appears to be little question of the fact, so far as these tests extend, that the parochial school children receive a broader social (awareness) education than the public school children."

Do Catholic schools really prepare students well for life? Do these students achieve economic success?

When the American Catholic Church made the decision to build a separate school system, most Catholics were very poor, and many of them were immigrants. Now, several generations later, what kind of an economic picture do we see?

Catholics have been climbing up the financial ladder of success, along with other Americans. They have moved into occupations with more prestige. In achieving both the money and the prestige, a Catholic-school education turned out to be an advantage over attending public schools.

In studying the economic impact of a Catholic education, the Greeley-Rossi team reported extremely interesting facts. Their data show that the more well-to-do a person's father was, the more likely this person was to have attended a Catholic school. (p. 278)

When Catholics achieve financial success, they seem more determined than ever to send their children to Catholic schools. Greeley and Rossi note that you might expect that as Catholics began to move up in society, they would have preferred to melt in with the general population of America. One way to do this would be to send their children to the public schools. Evidently many Catholics did not select this alternative. They remained loyal to their own schools to a significant degree, even as they did acquire more money and a higher social position in the community.

Concerning the relationship between religion and economics, recent studies of religious practice have shown that religiousness, as demonstrated by church attendance, does increase with social class.[35] Such facts would seem to offer comfort to Catholic educators. If more and more Catholics achieve economic success, then these Catholics, according to Greeley and Rossi, would tend to lend strong support to their schools.

Several cautious notes will have to be sounded here, however. There are other factors that might affect this picture. The serious cost increases now hitting Catholic schools could upset the trend noted by the sociologists. Ever since the Greeley-Rossi report was issued, the large number of sisters leaving religious communities has added to the financial problems. These withdrawals also tend to create a "crisis of confidence" on the part of parents. These parents might not be so willing to support Catholic schools staffed almost exclusively by lay teachers. This is an unwarranted reaction, perhaps, but psychologically an understandable one nonetheless.

The increasing respectability of secular ideas, discussed earlier, may affect the compulsion some parents feel to provide Catholic education for their children. It also may be that Greeley and Rossi documented a trend upward that was just about to peak and then level off or drop. (If someone had studied the upward trend of the stock market in the twenties, before "the crash," they might have predicted a continued upward spiral also!)

To summarize, it is true that a study of economic success among Catholics so far seems to indicate that as Catholics become more successful financially, they tend to prefer Catholic schools to a greater degree. Although these figures appear to be an optimistic sign for the future, other factors could interfere with this trend. (One should add that the concerned, Christ-like educator would not want to appeal exclusively to a mobile upper-middle class.)

Are Catholics (especially the educated ones) drifting away from their schools? Do they have serious doubts about the value of Catholic education, as many magazine and newspaper articles seem to suggest?

Some headlines would certainly indicate that many of the intellectuals in the Church no longer support Catholic schools. Once again, however, the Greeley-Rossi scientific data did not confirm this supposition. The facts gathered in their research show just the opposite: the better educated the head of the household is, the more likely the child is to be in a Catholic school. (p. 279)

To shed further light on this topic we must glance at a special "study-within-a-study" undertaken by these sociologists. Probably this part of the Greeley-Rossi survey provided the greatest surprise to me, personally. The so-called "*Commonweal* Survey" has significance in connection with the future of Catholic schools.

"The question of the Catholic elite remains. It is possible that, while the majority of the Catholics in the country are reasonably satisfied with the school system, there is a small but crucial minority which is strongly dissatisfied. To test this possibility we report here some data available from a random sample of the readership of *The Commonweal* magazine. *The Commonweal* is a favorite journal among liberal Catholics in America and has, in recent years, tended to be critical of Catholic education. We can reasonably assume that if there are any strong feelings against Catholic education, these feelings will be found in the sample of the readers of *The Commonweal*." (p. 212)

Here are some of the surprises uncovered by this special survey.

Commonweal readers are much more likely to send their children to Catholic schools than are Catholics in the general population. And *Com-*

monweal readers are more inclined than anyone in the general population to stress religious training in Catholic schools.

Commonweal readers are less concerned with discipline training. They are also less concerned with physical facilities, curriculum modifications, athletic programs, and cutting costs. They are, however, concerned with changes in teaching and classroom size.

Only 7 percent of the Commonweal readers feel that parents should have more to say about decision-making in Catholic schools. (This is certainly a surprising reaction from a group you would expect to be very vocal about more lay control of Catholic schools!)

It is true that the magazine's readers who do not send their children to Catholic schools are inclined to be extremely critical of these schools. Such critics especially stress the sometimes overcrowded Catholic classrooms compared to public-school class size. (Yet, interestingly, some scientific research indicates that there is no consistent relationship between small class-size and student achievement.) A thorough analysis in the Archdiocese of Boston, for example, found "higher achievement in classes of 35 or more children."[36]

Concerning the Commonweal study, Greeley and Rossi reach these basic conclusions: "The data reported in this chapter are somewhat paradoxical. They confirm the impression of many Catholic educators that Catholic education has never been more popular. . . . But as the Catholic population becomes better educated and more articulate, it will inevitably grow more concerned about what goes on in its schools, particularly about the qualifications of teachers and the overcrowding of classrooms." (p. 217)

**Is any specific level of education more effective
in inculcating religious values?
Is elementary education more effective and important
than high school or college in the child's formation?**
We noted earlier that most Protestant and Jewish Americans are sensitive to the issue of whether Catholic schools are divisive. The most sensitive issue for most Catholics themselves concerns the question: "Which level of Catholic education is most important?"

Do we dare neglect the elementary school when young personalities are developing? On the other hand, should the Church abandon a school program for high school students as they undergo the adolescent crisis? And, don't you have the best chance of all at the college level, when the student is mature enough to significantly absorb a valid value-system on which to build an adult life?

Piaget seems to indicate that the very young cannot absorb value systems and broad concepts like brotherhood. It is also often true that the adolescent is so troubled by his own inner turmoil and confusion that the search for values gets temporarily postponed.

We might ask ourselves the question Greeley and Rossi raise: "Is it possible for Roman Catholicism (or indeed, for any institution that is interested in value-oriented education) to concentrate its efforts at one educational level and obtain results which would eliminate the necessity of maintaining schools at other levels?" (p. 159)

Greeley and Rossi, unfortunately, say that if Catholic policy-makers would go into session and seek an answer to the above question, their research facts would indicate: "No particular level is more effective than any other." (p. 181)

Indeed, their data point to the opposite conclusion. For formal religious education to be effective, it must be a comprehensive educational program. It must span all grades. In addition, this collective Catholic educational preparation probably will have the greatest impact on those who have also gone to a religious college.

It is an interesting research fact that the Catholic-college graduate who also attended a Catholic grammar school and a Catholic high school is most likely to be notably more religious; he is also most likely to be much more open and tolerant than Catholics without this comprehensive Catholic education.

Are all the changes within the Church since the Ecumenical Council having any real effect on Catholic education?

Throughout *The Flickering Light*, our primary emphasis is viewing Catholic schools of today, and asking whether these schools will, or should, be around tomorrow. Except for our brief historical treatment of the development of Catholic schools, our chief concern is the present and the future in Catholic education.

We must remind ourselves, therefore, that here in the Greeley-Rossi survey we are primarily focusing upon what Catholic education has been in the *past*. Most of the adults questioned for this study had attended Catholic schools sometime between five and fifty-five years previously (between 1910 and 1960).

The important questions are: Have Catholic schools changed in very recent years? When Pope John opened his window to let some fresh air into the Church, did this fresh air reach, and affect, Catholic school classrooms? If research studies were conducted now, or within another five to ten years, is it possible that the results would be dramatically different, given this post-Vatican II emphasis?

These questions are more difficult to answer than all of the others investigated, because we are dealing with changes that are so recent. It will take some time (and more research) to give valid information on this matter.

To attempt to get some answers, Greeley and Rossi left questionnaires with the adults they surveyed. These special forms were not filled out by the parents, however, but by the adolescent children of these adults. With these answers, the social scientists concluded the following.

In today's Catholic-school student there are much stronger associations between religious behavior and their education than were observed in the adult respondents. Thus, current Catholic educational practices seem to effect more dramatic and valid religious growth. The immediate strength of these associations probably would be eroded somewhat as time goes by, however.

Greeley also noted that those in Catholic schools at the time of the study seemed much more academically oriented than Catholics in public schools, and even more so than Protestants in public schools.

And, finally, the view of adolescents in Catholic schools in 1965 indicated that there was no substantiation for the notion that Catholic schools were more likely to be "unfair" or "authoritarian." (pp. 197-198)

Catholic education's past clearly reflects the posture of a "ghetto church"—generally protective, stressing basic religious facts and orthodox information. This has been the thrust of the Catholic educational approach until recently. Therefore, graduates from Catholic schools in the past probably would reflect a stress upon a legalistic attitude rather than a sensitive social outlook. This is unfortunate, but it reflects the defensive attitude which the Church adopted, or was forced to adopt, for previous generations.

Hopefully, innovative and imaginative Catholic educational programs of the present and the future will help to produce a Catholic-school graduate with a different profile. I don't know that this will happen, and I certainly can't guarantee that Catholic education will provide these new educational approaches. I simply want to point out that if Catholic schools are still healthy and strong in twenty years, and if they are surveyed periodically during that period, we might have a different—and more hopeful—set of statistics for Catholic-school graduates who had the advantages of the Ecumenical Council and its effect on Catholic education.

To state an "ecumenical I.Q." for past Catholic-school graduates is rather unfair. The spirit of ecumenism in the Catholic Church is a relatively recent development. This factor is an example of the need for continued meaningful research in Catholic education. As cultures and Catholic viewpoints change, Catholic schools and Catholic-school graduates should certainly reflect this change.

Greeley-Rossi Confidence

The Greeley-Rossi research asked some very basic questions. The research scientists got answers, but not all of the answers were perfectly pat ones.

Mature sociologists, along with everyone else, realize that most things are not completely black or white, but various shades of gray.

There are some shades of gray in the Greeley-Rossi results. However, these authors provided the first major scientific analysis of Catholic-school graduates. All educators and parents—Catholic, Protestant and Jewish—are indebted to them for this significant research. Any projected planning for the future of Catholic schools in America must build upon this and similar scientific structures.

When the Greeley-Rossi report was issued, the writers seemed certain that Catholic schools were here to stay. The sociologists were commenting scientifically on the Catholic school strengths at that time. They were not, essentially, asking *whether* Catholic schools *should* stay. Readers could sense hopeful optimism in this statement: "Our opinion, for what it is worth, is that discussion by Catholics and non-Catholics alike concerning whether there will be Catholic schools is quite irrelevant. A system which involves one out of every seven school children in our republic does not go out of business, either all at once or gradually. It seems to us, rather, that the relevant question is how the distinctive system of Catholic schools can make the strongest possible contribution to the health of American society . . . Being for or against a school system with over five million students is like being for or against the Rocky Mountains; it's great fun but it does not notably alter the reality."[37]

In 1970, just four years after the Greeley-Rossi research publication date, Andrew Greeley co-authored a book entitled *Can Catholic Schools Survive?*[38] That title certainly doesn't exude the confidence noted in the above Greeley-Rossi conclusion. Much has happened in just four years. As we mentioned earlier, Catholic schools, like many other solid institutions, have been chewed up by change.

Greeley, as sociologist, in his new book, answers the question posed by the book's title. He says Catholics are discussing whether or not Catholic schools are possible and should exist. Again he questions the relevance of such inquiries. "While both issues have considerable theoretical interest and can present challenges to wit and ingenuity at liberal Catholic . . . parties, they are both ultimately unresolved and irrelevant. Catholic schools do exist. They are not going to be eliminated, if only because the pressures on the public school systems in the large metropolitan centers in the northeast and north central sections of the country make such elimination inconceivable."[39]

Greeley, the educator, also comments upon the Catholic-school performance record in this 1970 volume. "All data available indicate that Catholic schools are on the average somewhat superior academically to public schools. Catholic secondary schools are considerably superior to public high schools."

A NEW THEOLOGY OF CATHOLIC EDUCATION

Four years after his initial research analysis, Greeley felt that a bold new statement of purpose for Catholic schools was necessary to bolster the sagging, almost suicidal, morale among Catholic educators entering the decade of the seventies. In this analysis, Fr. Andrew Greeley adds his dimension as a priest to his sociological and educational expertise.

He notes that theology and sociology have both contributed to the current confusion. "The answer is reasonably simple. Catholic schools, like the rest of the American Church, have been caught in the currents and countercurrents stirred up by the intersection of two transitions, from Counter-Reformation to Ecumenical Age, and from immigrant slum to professional suburbs."[40]

The transition from the defensive, protective, ghetto mentality to the openness of ecumenism is a difficult one. It is made even more difficult because the transition has occurred so rapidly. This is why a new rationale is missing. Greeley sketches an outline for this new theology of education, hoping others—"professional theologians"—will strengthen it.

His strongest statement concerning purpose is: "Now it seems safe to assume that education is one of the most important cultural activities in which men engage, for through the educational process they try to pass on their culture to the generation after them and also to expand and enrich the cultural heritage. If the Church is committed to the role of leader of man's pilgrimage, it seems appropriate, though surely not absolutely necessary, that the Church be involved in education, not to defend or protect the faith of its members, but to bear witness to its conviction of mankind's destiny by taking the lead in mankind's educational progress. So an appropriate goal for Catholic education would be the task of 'research and development.' Catholic educators should be leaders in educational innovation."[41]

Two other ingredients must be included in our new vision, according to Greeley: love and laughter. ". . . Because of the Church's commitment to love, the teachers in Catholic schools ought to be better lovers . . ."[42] Comedy is necessary because "one of the most dramatic cultural changes of our time is the attempt of increasing numbers of American people to deal with the rationalized, computerized, bureaucratized, formalized, secularized society in which they live."[43]

In evaluating this recent analysis of Catholic schools' chances of survival, one writer sums up Greeley's current message. "Catholic schools are very much worth saving, and can not only survive but grow and thrive—if only we have the will. We have everything else we need, contrary to all prophets of doom. What we badly need is less gloom and more courage and charisma."[44]

In 1972 Catholic research was enriched as another scientific study emerged through the efforts of the priest-sociologist, Andrew M. Greeley. While not as directly related to the educational scene as his Catholic school study, this new research reflects both problems and promises for Catholic educators.

Greeley provides a study summary in *Priests in the United States: Reflections on a Survey.* This volume also includes his personal speculation and recommendations, based on the data gathered from 5,155 priests, 750 former priests, 165 bishops, and 155 religious order superiors.

The priesthood study was commissioned by the American bishops. Complete research reports are contained in two volumes:

The Catholic Priest in the United States: Sociological Investigations, by Andrew M. Greeley, U.S. Catholic Conference, 476 p, $8.95

The Catholic Priest in the United States: Psychological Investigations, by Eugene C. Kennedy and Victor J. Heckler, U.S. Catholic Conference, 271 p, $7.95

Significant for our Catholic school analysis are Greeley's findings concerning clergy support for Catholic schools. "It is interesting to note from our data that only 20 percent of the diocesan priests and 17 percent of the active priests are in favor of the elimination of Catholic schools. Sixty-nine percent of the priests under thirty-five and 77 percent of those between thirty-six and forty-five are not willing to agree to the elimination of the Catholic school systems." (p. 113) As Greeley rather sharply indicates, this data does *not* support the idea that American clergy no longer want Catholic schools. However, there are indications in this study that in several key areas, potential threats to the system do exist.

One such realistic assessment concerns manpower, or personnel recruitment. Greeley presents a valuable analysis of the problem of recruiting applicants to the priesthood. This data would probably also apply to the religious orders of nuns and brothers staffing Catholic schools.

Greeley warns there is no reason to think the resignation rate will taper off. Even more ominous (for Catholic school administrators) is the fact that the numbers entering religious life have seriously declined. The study points to the chief reason for this decline: men in the priesthood today show a lack of enthusiasm in recruiting youth to their own life style.

Today's clergy are struggling through adaptations and changes in the priesthood. For this reason, many priests hesitate urging young men to join their ranks. This is a very serious threat to continued growth in the apostolic work of the Church, unless competent laity are organized to assist in these endeavors.

Greeley editorializes: "In the long run, only the reorganization of church structures and the effective reformulation of the Christian message will attract more young men to the ministry."

Greeley summarizes his own optimism and pessimism, both interpreted in the light of the priesthood study data. Pessimism is dictated by the resignation rate; the lack of enthusiastic recruiting among the priests themselves; the strain between priests and their leaders; and the differences between younger and older clergy, along with the fact that some priests are discouraged or fail to feel challenged in their work.

Again editorializing, the priest-sociologist adds his own personal reflections concerning the quality of Church leadership and the potential loss of valuable traditions through confusion and uncertainty. He specifically mentions that "the immensely important Catholic school system" is threatened by this confusion.

Greeley adds, however, that some of the survey staff were, themselves, surprised at the signs of strength which give grounds for optimism. "We did not discover emotional immaturity among priests when they were compared with other groups of typical American males." And "the morale of priests is quite high, higher indeed than that of typical American males of the same age and the same educational background."

Like the Greeley-Rossi study, these facts can either be assimilated by Catholic educational leaders, or they can be ignored. In a real way, however, the Catholic schools of America are seriously threatened if such research results are ignored.

PATTERNS OF DIVERSITY

The validity of the nonpublic school as an alternative choice for American families has received substantial support from the highly-respected academic analysis published recently by The Johns Hopkins University Press. Entitled *American Nonpublic Schools, Patterns of Diversity*, the volume is authored by Otto F. Kraushaar, who has served as a Research Associate of Harvard's Graduate School of Education. Dr. Kraushaar has also been on the staffs of Smith College, the University of Iowa, and Goucher College.

Supporting this research were individuals long associated with educational excellence and innovation. Kraushaar acknowledges aid from many sources. Among them: the National Association of Independent Schools; The National Catholic Education Association; Danforth, Carnegie, and Ford Foundations; and Dr. Theodore Sizer, formerly Dean of the Harvard Graduate School of Education.

Some time ago, *America* magazine editorialized the theme of *choice*: ". . . what we really need is . . . an adequate *diversity* of (educational) opportunity." And Kraushaar's theme can be summed up in the simple word *alternatives*.

The point of this book is not to argue the superiority of private over public schools, but rather to defend the dual system of private *and* public schools . . . It seems obvious that for the public schools to acquire a virtual monopoly in educating the young would be a major social disaster. As public institutions become ever more impersonal and grow out of scale with people, the need for alternatives, choices, and options increases.

Kraushaar later notes that while nonpublic schools are privately managed, they are essentially public in function. (This public service offered by nonpublic schools is one of the reasons for nonpublic school claims upon public funds.)

Kraushaar's study of the nonpublic school has three thrusts. Part I is introductory, giving the historical circumstances under which nonpublic schools arose. Part II, based on questionnaires, interviews and school visits, moves within nonpublic schools. Topics analyzed include the emerging student outlook, faculty, administration, finances, racial questions, and the challenge of institutional change. Part III is "an effort to grapple with the major issues of public policy regarding nonpublic schools and to assess the changing role of private schooling as it affects the prospects of nonpublic schools of all types."

In the book's Appendix, Kraushaar again repeats the theme supporting the study's research plan. ". . . Schooling serves the ends of individuals and society best if it provides a variety of goals and methods among which persons may choose. The study does not aim, therefore, to identify a single type of institution which could serve as a model for private or for public schools; it aims instead to trace the effects of voluntary choice in schooling and its implications for educational practice and theory."

The term "nonpublic school," therefore, embraces a variety of educational approaches. Included in Kraushaar's "diversity" are Catholic schools, Protestant church-affiliated schools, independent schools, and Jewish schools. (Not included are vocational schools or schools offering only kindergarten or the first five grades.)

About 77 percent of all nonpublic schools are Catholic schools. Therefore, there is much valuable scientific data in Kraushaar's study for Catholic educational leaders to integrate into their own educational planning and administration. Kraushaar structured his sampling, however, so the research would not merely be an investigation of Catholic schools. Both in his questionnaire surveys and in the schools visited, the aim was to show the wide diversity of educational options available in nonpublic schools.

Survey instruments consisted of five different questionnaires directed at administrators, the faculty, the students, and parents and governing boards. In addition, Kraushaar's staff distributed a general questionnaire about the school covering topics such as school government, curriculum, accreditation, faculty background, finances, and the composition of the student body.

Kraushaar's work is literally a gold mine of scientific material which, added to the earlier Greeley-Rossi data, provides hard facts for Catholic education in the seventies. It is impossible to summarize all the appropriate material but here is just a sample of some significant findings.

The broad religious community still serves many Americans as the primary context of self-identification and social belonging. However, support for Catholic schools (and all nonpublic schools) will be forthcoming only as long as the family is satisfied with the school. At the present time, most parents are satisfied with their choice of a nonpublic school. (87 to 100 percent in the various groups said they would enroll their child in the school if they had it to do over again.) The great majority of nonpublic school students are also satisfied with their school. These students are also convinced they receive more attention than they would in a public school. Catholic school parents appreciate an academically challenging curriculum, but feel this is not to be preferred above an education in religiously rooted values.

Contrary to the prevailing impression of many intellectuals, who in the past consistently underestimated the quality of the educational output of Catholic schools, there is among these institutions a rising potential for innovation and reform. Most people agree that one of the most valuable services private schools can render is to innovate—to demonstrate new and better ways. New York Times Education Editor, Fred Hechinger, states: "The fact is that the public schools need—and need desperately— the free-wheeling presence of the independent schools."

For example, the Catholic school system is in a unique position to play a major role in the integration of American schools. The United States Office of Education reported that in 1970-71, 38 percent of all black children enrolled in Catholic schools were not themselves Catholic. (New York Times, April 7, 1971.)

There is a new trend in nonpublic education toward community schools functioning as humanistic educational laboratories. Some are in storefronts; and some are in priority inner city Catholic schools. However, Kraushaar, along with Jencks and Greeley-Rossi, reinforce the concept that schools, including nonpublic schools, bring limited influence on the child's achievement that is independent of his background and social context.

Students, themselves, say they want most of all to have the school assist them "to learn to think clearly and independently." Catholic-school students cite stronger moral education as the greatest benefit that Catholic schools can confer. Kraushaar challenges that the time has come for public and nonpublic school staffs to work together "with full and sympathetic understanding" on matters such as dual enrollment, and other educational innovations.

Concerning Catholic school economics, Kraushaar documents that well over three-fourths of the Catholic school heads characterize their students as middle class or lower (and more than half of all Catholic schools reported having students from families at or below the poverty level). The weight of evidence shows "beyond a reasonable doubt that the cost of nonpublic education now exceeds the combined resources of individual and organized private support." These nonpublic school financial problems require: long-range planning, budgets; more cooperation between schools; serious student recruitment efforts; fund raising, and imaginative financial leadership.

Change has quickly enveloped nonpublic schools in America. Kraushaar documents the effects of this change and the attempts to manage it. If the financial crisis can be solved, and nonpublic schools can maintain the confidence of American parents and students, Kraushaar's research points to exciting opportunities for Americans in their attempt to provide "patterns of diversity."

CONCLUSION

We have seen, briefly, the historical development of a separate Catholic school system in America—established by lay leadership, designed by the hierarchy, sustained by the sacrifice of those who staffed them, and patronized by the laity who sent their children to them and paid the bills.

The philosophy and theology of Catholic education have been explored, along with its special view of man and the significant role religious thought and action play in the Christian's life.

And, finally, we have listened to the social scientists. Their data have indicated that there is a moderate, but significant association between Catholic education and adult religious behavior. This association is strongest among those who come from very religious backgrounds. The association seems to be affected also by cumulative attendance at Catholic schools, from the elementary level through the Catholic college.

However, there were only very weak associations between Catholic school attendance and enlightened social attitudes. Little relationship could be found between religious behavior and attending Confraternity of Christian Doctrine (CCD or "Sunday School" classes). There is no evidence that Catholic schools have been absolutely necessary for the survival of American Catholicism.

With all this already said, we must squarely face the question with which this section opened: "Should Catholic schools close?"

There are two extreme answers to this question.

One may suggest, for example, that we carry into the future the same program we embraced in the past. This alternative is clearly impossible.

We have vastly different circumstances in Catholic schools today. These circumstances force change upon the Church. Decreasing vocations, increased lay-teacher costs, and other factors discussed earlier simply mean that we can never return to the standard approaches we lived with before. We are now in a new era, and we must have new concepts in Catholic education to reflect this fact.

The opposite extreme is to tear the whole structure down and begin all over again. As many other writers have commented, this solution is not very practical either. Koob and Shaw recently stated: "If the [Catholic] schools should disappear, there is nothing even remotely visible on the horizon that could take their place."[45]

The same attitude haunts us from the pages of the Greeley-Rossi report. "Has it been worth all the time, money and effort? . . . We suggest that a more relevant question is whether there exists at the present time an alternative institution which would accomplish the same goals with less expenditure. Our data suggest that CCD programs will need major improvement before they can be seriously considered as a functional alternative."[46] (Some Catholics have urged such massive funding to improve these religious education programs. However, the closing of schools won't automatically insure CCD success. Recently, Pueblo, Colo. closed all their schools and designed a big CCD thrust. A recent statement there decried "the impossible situation" which, it claimed, was the result of apathy.)

This "let's-tear-it-all-down-and-begin-anew" approach seems severe and impractical. One problem is that this approach assumes a grave risk. What if you abandon the whole system for something else, and then the new approach isn't as effective as the system you have just dismantled? Then it's too late; you've already destroyed the structure to test your hunch that you'd get along better without it.

This may not be as unrealistic as it sounds. The newsletter *Overview*, which usually reflects a liberal viewpoint, editorialized: "Catholics who reason that we should phase out parochial schools and give children their religious education in CCD classes might find reason for reconsidering their position in a report by Chicago *Daily News* religion editor, James H. Bowman, who reveals that many Protestant leaders are disillusioned with the current state of Sunday schools and [are] "convinced they are a waste of time." Rev. Dr. Taylor McConnell, Garrett Theological Seminary professor of Christian education, claims that "Sunday schools are very sick, and they've been sick for a number of years."[47]

One active Protestant layman confided to this author: "Most Protestant Sunday school programs are a joke. They certainly are not effective educationally."

Liberals who are honestly seeking a new and better approach for Catholic education must also guard against being too dogmatic in their liberalism. The Church has been criticized in the past for issuing commands and expecting automatic and unquestioning obedience. Today Church leaders are agonizing through the authority question to determine just how such authority can be shared effectively. While liberals rejoice at the concept of the Catholic Church becoming more democratic, liberals themselves must guard against becoming undemocratic in their pronouncements.

A noted Catholic layman has rather ironically indicted such edicts.

I get the feeling that the Pope isn't infallible and the Council isn't, but half the Catholics I meet are. [48]

There are, therefore, two different suggestions for solving Catholic educational problems: to make no changes, or to close the whole system down. Both solutions are extreme. And those who embrace these extreme positions often feel so strongly their solution is the correct one that they object to any deviation from their stand.

I have come to think that the most meaningful solution for the present falls somewhere in between these two extremes. Most administrators, teachers, and parents realize that some change and adaptation is necessary, but they do not want to throw out the whole system until there are reasonable alternatives to take its place. We shall explore some of these alternatives in Part III.

SUMMARY

Problems and Promises: American Catholic Schools

A beautiful challenge to Catholic educators has been stated by a modern woman who does not, herself, run schools, but whose whole life is a lesson. Mother Teresa of Calcutta has said: "The biggest disease today is not leprosy or tuberculosis, but rather the feeling of being unwanted, uncared for and deserted by everybody. The greatest evil is the lack of love and charity, the terrible indifference towards one's neighbour who lives at the roadside assaulted by exploitation, corruption, poverty and disease."

After several years of research and evaluation, I have reached the conclusion that there *is* a definite need for an *alternative* educational system in America. The question of who is to administer these schools is still open, with more responsibility moving to parents and the laity, as religious vocations decline. Gabriel Moran, FSC, noted: "The Church ought not to 'run schools': it ought to *be* a center of education, a community to which experience is ordered on a knowing basis. It ought to deal with the profoundest experiences and the questioning of experience that men freely bring to it."

Catholic schools face problems and promises. . . . As we have noted, there are various threads running through the fabric of Catholic education at the present time. These patterns or trends result from varied causes.

1. Increased costs are the direct result of inflation and higher salaries for increasing numbers of lay teachers.
2. Changes have occurred within religious communities, demonstrated to the public by the new "habit" and a new life-style for nuns.
3. Theological renewal and the re-evaluation of church priorities were synthesized by the Vatican Council.
4. The social status of American Catholics has altered; Catholics are no longer defensively gathered in ethnic ghettos.
5. Upheavals have occurred in society, such as the rapid rate of change documented by Toffler in *Future Shock*.

As a result of the above upheavals, Catholics have heard arguments advanced for closing schools.

1. It is disproportionate to spend so much money on a program reaching a small percentage of the total Catholic population.
2. The proper role of the Church is to teach the people their needs through Gospel witness. Buildings and institutions often detract from emphasis upon this fundamental mission.

One of America's great superintendents of schools, Gregory Coffin, formerly of Evanston, Illinois, pointed out that three of the men who most radically shaped current American attitudes have been clergy: Pope John XXIII, Martin Luther King, Jr., and Malcolm X. I believe the people of God will remain deeply engaged in the educational enterprise—in terms of public policy, and in offering "school" experiences.

And the promises . . .

● ● ● An organized school program still seems the most effective vehicle for integrating Christian values with all of learning. However, this structured program will probably reach out more than it has in the past—to parents, to the community, and to the modern world.

- - - In the Church's educational mission, a better balance must be effected between Catholic schools, CCD programs, adult education, youth programs, and work with senior citizens. All of these groups constitute the people of God on pilgrimage; all must share the educational resources of a laboratory for Christian living.
- - - Catholic educational programs—in schools and in resource centers and in communications—must represent *excellence*. An alternative that is second rate simply will not be chosen by American Catholics today.
- - - Faith and commitment built an educational operation under Catholic auspices in America; this same dedication is required in the process of reassessing the system, consolidating it, and restructuring it for the future.
- - - Financial reorganization will be required to achieve these educational objectives. New approaches will be tried: new forms of aid to schools; diocesan reorganization; and more lay fiscal responsibility and control.
- - - One of the crucial challenges facing America's Catholic schools at the present time is the need to formulate and demonstrate goals that are clarified. All Catholic educational programs must define and communicate their goals and objectives, and they must communicate with their clientele to assess their own needs.

PART III

What are the alternatives?

How long ago did you buy a new piece of furniture? When did you last purchase a TV set? Do you have a washing machine or a drier? How often do you trade in your car?

These questions may give you an idea of how the obsolescence factor affects your life as a consumer. Very few cars will last ten years. You may even be forced to turn yours in before you make the last payment on it. And your washing machine isn't made to last forever either. Our "modern conveniences" self-destruct very quickly, and consumers are pressured into buying more up-to-date models.

What about the obsolescence factor in education? Isn't it important to keep your child's educational experience as up-to-date as your automobile? If you don't expect your car to last forever, doesn't it make sense that teaching techniques become old-fashioned too? Maybe today's children are getting a "Model T" education. This will never equip them for life in an age of jets and aerospace discoveries.

You would like to drive a safe automobile; what about educational safety? How can your children be protected from educational accidents, and even casualties? The obsolescence factor affects all public-school classrooms. Catholic educators, too, must conduct an "examination of conscience" regarding this preparation for the future. Are Catholics and their schools ready for the twenty-first century? Are they even relevant to this decade? That's what this part of *The Flickering Light* is all about.

CAN RELIGIOUS SCHOOLS BE RELEVANT?

There is a certain irony in these questions: "Should Catholic schools close?" or "Can a relevant Catholic-school service exist in America?"

The first ironic thing is that the questions are raised seriously by Catholics themselves—often by priests, brothers, sisters, and laity who are a part of the present Catholic-school structure. But perhaps it takes someone who really loves Catholic education to have the courage to cite its shortcomings, and seek solutions to them including considering a whole new approach. As it stands, Catholic educators could chorus the ecology bumper-stickers that read: "We have found the enemy, and it is us."

Most of the people who are unhappy with Catholic schools today say the problem with parochial education is that it is old. "Old" may mean "venerable" in some cultures, but not in our fast-paced American lifestyle. Such commentators are disturbed because they feel Catholic schools have a nineteenth-century approach to twentieth-century problems. (A friend of mine, however, has suggested that 'Catholic' education should be *timeless*, not just timely. While up-dating has value, Catholic education should go *beyond* this.)

The second ironic aspect of the situation is this: just when Catholic schools are receiving the kind of abrasive evaluation that could renew many schools, some critics ask not for renewal, but for abolition. Why must the only solution for an out-of-date school be to close the school? What about *changing* the school? Why not consider improving the school to make it timely? Many urban public schools are inadequate, but no one suggests closing the whole system down; the challenge, in many instances, is to improve such a system by trying new approaches, rather than shutting it off completely. Some experts urge us to look beyond the school to the problem of *parish* renewal.

A personal note must be inserted here before we look at specific details of some alternative approaches for Catholic education in the years ahead. In appealing to reason, rather than emotion, in our discussion of whether Catholic schools should close or change, I do not mean to imply that all of us are computers, devoid of emotion. Given our personal "hangups," it is difficult to be completely objective.

We should bring out into the open the question of my own "prejudice." I have been a professional administrator in the Catholic educational system for over ten years. Is it possible for me to evaluate and criticize this structure while being part of it?

Frankly, it's impossible for a person to guarantee complete openness. However, I have conscientiously aimed for such openness.

I have tried, with integrity, to write an open book—one that is reaching out to seek an educational program to help our culture, our country, and the human beings who constitute the Church. This book has not been written as a defense for Catholic schools. The book, instead, raises questions and seeks answers. As a matter of fact, when starting this book I did not have an air-tight little "case" for, or against, Catholic schools in my head to pass along to others. I have, quite honestly, sought solutions as my research and writing developed over several years.

In seeking these answers to existing Catholic-school problems, there are two basic avenues to explore. First we have the practical questions: how much will changes and improvements cost and where will the money come from? These financial matters must be faced. They won't go away if they are ignored.

The other avenue is probably more significant when seeking these solutions, however. And that is: if you had the money, exactly what would you do with it? What *specific* reforms would make Catholic education in America more relevant to today's needs?

We will travel down each of these roads—exploring the financial problem, along with the specific reforms or alternatives the funds (if obtained) should finance.

FINANCIAL FACTS

In 1971, according to Dr. George Elford, total church expenditures amounted to $406 million for elementary schools and $81 million for high schools.

There is a concept abroad in Catholic circles that if state and federal funding were only permitted by the United States Supreme Court, problems facing Catholic schools would be solved.

Nothing could be further from the truth! Money is important. However, it is not the only important thing in Catholic education; in the long run it probably is not the most important factor. The varied challenges facing Catholic schools would not be solved if they had a blank check from the federal government. And, given the present mood of the Supreme Court, they are not likely to get such blank checks.

An interesting analysis of the "myth of money" appeared as a *Saturday Review* cover story (July, 1972), entitled "Can Catholic Schools Stay Afloat?"

One of the article's authors, Louis R. Gary, served as a consultant to President Nixon's Commission on School Finance. Gary notes that factors forcing enrollment declines include:

- • • Catholic schools are beginning to reflect the recent drop in birth rates
- • • Some Catholic parents are simply choosing *not* to send their child to a Catholic school
- • • Many Catholic schools are losing their distinctiveness

(The final reason cited recalls the advice of a noted educational innovator, Dr. Dwight W. Allen, Dean of the School of Education at the University of Massachusetts. Often cited for his "radical" ideas, Dr. Allen recently noted that Catholic education is losing its sense of Christian purpose in an attempt to "ape" public education. Criticizing this attempt to gain an image of "with-it-ness," Dr. Allen added that to try innovations in a school which has lost its sense of purpose is mere "window-dressing." Dr. Allen called for an end to neutrality in schools. "I want teachers who are committed to a value system, who are partisan, who are biased.")

Louis Gary notes that "academically . . . Catholic schools are as good as public schools—if not better." But, he adds, the schools are caught in ideological conflicts in the church itself.

The need for self-help is underscored also by the President's Panel on Nonpublic Education in its report *Nonpublic Education and the Public Good.* The panel notes that at no time did the commission entertain the notion that nonpublic schools would be, or should be, rescued totally by a public effort.

The commission adds a sobering note:

The stark fact is this: given the enormous demands on the public purse, no government instrumentality is able to provide full funding for private educational ventures over the next critical five-year period.

Panel members remind nonpublic school educators and parents: "The maxim that 'God helps those who help themselves' has this secular varient: 'When the going gets tough, the tough get going' ".

The Nixon Commission on School Finance, New York's controversial Fleischmann Report, and many other educational analysts are stressing a similar theme—if Catholics want to preserve a school system in America, they must work hard to preserve it (just as Catholics worked hard to build it in the first place).

Catholics cannot simply work hard for some form of aid. This is not enough. As our consolidation section notes, Gary has here issued a warning on the need for a massive consolidation of Catholic schools. He has urged church leaders to *preserve the option* of Catholic education itself, rather than trying exclusively for school aid, or to preserve buildings.

On the local level, many schools are, for the first time, beginning an active recruitment plan. If support is faltering in some areas, it could well be that parents are worried about enrolling children because they feel the school may later close.

For Catholic schools a seller's market has ended. The President's Commissions remind Catholic schools of this. "Parents who, a few years ago, were willing to pay a premium to enroll their children in a nonpublic school are 'shopping' for the best school. It is now a buyer's market where children will be in short supply to a degree contradicting predictions made only three or four years ago. Most institutions will have to move competitively to maintain their membership."

It has never been easy to maintain a Catholic school system. It still isn't easy.

It *does* appear some form of financial aid is necessary for the survival of Catholic schools, as we have known them. But even if, and when, such aid is received, there would remain special questions and problems for Catholic educators. And some new difficulties will be added to our present problems, if Catholic schools accept any kind of aid, for with funds will come restrictions and controls.

There are some questions that cannot be answered solely by money. How can we develop a social conscience among Catholic-school graduates? What is the best way to provide innovative professional approaches to religious education, within schools or outside of them? Can we safeguard the basic moral and Christian humanistic outlook that should be reflected in Catholic classrooms? Is it possible to train students to think for themselves, instead of merely absorbing spoon-fed rote religious learning? How can the educational generation gap be lessened, so youthful idealists can work well with matured professionals? Not all of these challenges will be met exclusively by the ring of the cash register.

First we should estimate the amount of money required for present and new approaches to Catholic education. Then we must discuss funding sources available.

President Nixon has said: "If most or all private schools were to close or turn public, the added burden on public funds by the end of the 1970s would exceed $4 billion per year in operations, with an estimated $5 billion more needed for facilities."[1]

The education of each child in a Catholic-school elementary classroom during the 1969-1970 school year cost $200.[2] Thus, the annual school bill for Catholics as the decade opened was $1.4 billion dollars. Now, we are talking about a different amount if all these children were to be absorbed into public schools because the per capita cost is higher in public school classrooms ($722 per pupil instead of $200), as President Nixon noted. By 1971-72, the elementary per pupil cost had increased only $68 per year in Catholic schools.

This cost would amount to $4 billion per year to U.S. public schools if all Catholic schools were to close. Added to that figure would be $5 billion on a one-time basis for the cost of providing the extra classrooms to absorb the new students. This would require new buildings in many areas, or the purchase or lease of existing buildings from Catholic-school authorities.

By the 1971-72 school year, without capital expenditures, it cost $268 per year to educate a student in a Catholic elementary school. Catholic high school students cost $531 per year. And private academy costs averaged $669 per pupil per year.

Like other aspects of life today—where changes occur almost before we are aware of them—the financial stability of Catholic schools seemed altered almost overnight. Many people remember the time, not too long ago, when new Catholic schools were opening every year, and it seemed as if continued growth and expansion lay ahead.

What happened? The financial crisis can be understood chiefly by explaining the increased dependence upon lay teachers in the Catholic schools throughout America. This, more than any other factor, created an economic impasse. A lay teacher does not live within the context of a religious congregation. Therefore, in terms of simple justice, lay teachers require a "living wage." This is not to say that lay teachers are not good for Catholic schools; it simply indicates that they cost a great deal more money than a teaching sister in the same classroom.

There is no doubt that it would have been impossible to build the Catholic-school structure in America without the use of the priests, sisters, and brothers. In 1940, or 1950, for example, if a parish decided to build a school, the people had to raise the money for the buildings (usually a school and a convent) and that was it. There were many teachers available since many youth were entering religious life. So the pastor and his people raised the money (or borrowed it), built the buildings, and then arranged to get a small group of nuns to come live in the convent and teach in the school. Once these initial investments were made, the on-going expense of maintaining a parish school was about manageable.

The parish provided living quarters for the sisters, but even so, without the very low-cost labor of such sisters, priests, and brothers, it simply would have been impossible for Catholics to build a huge educational structure like the one they erected in America.

Recently a research study was conducted of two urban dioceses, one in the Midwest and one on the Pacific coast. The value of services contributed to the parishes by religious teachers in one diocese averaged $5,425 per teacher per year. In the other diocese, the contribution averaged $3,572 per year per teacher.[3]

As the lay-teacher percentage increases on Catholic-school faculties, these savings disappear. And lay teachers now outnumber religious teachers in Catholic elementary and secondary schools. The New York Archdiocese and the Brooklyn Diocese report that the number of lay teachers has passed 50 percent. The National Catholic Educational Association says more than 25 other major school systems have a majority of lay faculty. Nationally, NCEA reported 80,200 lay teachers in the 1969-70 school year. [4] The 1969-70 ratio was 51 sisters to 49 lay teachers, nationally. Only two years previously (1967-68), the ratio was 62 sisters to 38 lay teachers. The 1972 National Catholic Directory notes that of a total of 188,527 teachers in Catholic schools, 104,236 are now lay teachers.

Suppose a parish had a school in 1950 with eight grades and two classrooms per grade. This means the parish had to support sixteen teachers. If these teachers were all nuns, the parish paid a small stipend for each teacher and provided a convent for the group to live in. By 1965, with decreasing numbers entering religious life and with additional numbers of sisters deciding to leave it, this parish school would have changed. There might now be only eight sisters available to assign to this school. This means that the other eight classrooms would now have lay teachers in them, or would be empty of both teachers and students. Suppose the salary paid to lay teachers was only $5,000. As a result, the parish must somehow provide almost $50,000 per year for its lay teachers, while still supporting the sisters who remained. Faced with such an annual expense, many parishes cut back on the number of classes in the school, to cut down on the need for teachers. As the decade of the seventies began, the average elementary school salary in Catholic schools was $5,575. High school salaries were about $8,000. If such a pastor eliminated grades seven and eight in the Catholic school, he could save $12,000 per year in lay-teacher salaries. So the great cut-back got underway.

And a full-fledged financial crisis began mounting within Catholic schools. By the 1970-71 school year, the average salary for lay teachers in Catholic elementary schools was $5,575, and for high schools, approximately $8,000.

Some writers feel that the Church is approaching a saturation point in terms of financial support from Catholics themselves. However, one observer, who we shall discuss shortly, disagrees strongly with this analysis.

In noting that there is decreasing enthusiasm for Catholic schools, many analysts could be misinterpreting the present scene. Polls generally have shown that large numbers of Catholic parents still prefer to send their children to a Catholic school—provided a school is available and the cost is reasonable.

In Brooklyn, "a lopsided 81 percent majority responding to a diocesan 'opinionaire', favored continued operation of the diocesan grade and high school system."[5] In Pittsburgh the diocesan Education Study Commission received the same mandate.[6]

A recent Gallup Opinion Poll indicated that 70 percent of America's Catholics would prefer to give their children a Catholic education. [7] However, when Catholic school tuitions soar—as they have—many parents will conclude that they can no longer afford it. This does not necessarily mean the parents do not prefer a Catholic school; it simply becomes impractical because the school has priced itself out of the middle-class market. Also, such a cost-crisis can force schools to cut back on *quality* by eliminating special educational programs. If the quality of education suffers this could have an effect on the popularity of private schools too.

One observer summarized the financial squeeze in one sentence. "Recent figures have shown that parish income has increased 15 percent in the last five years, while school costs have increased 70 percent."[8] Obviously this high cost is a key factor in the growing restlessness felt by Catholics over their schools. Parents may still prefer the Catholic school, however, while rebelling against the high price tag.

The higher tuitions scare Catholic parents, but non-Catholic citizens, too, are appalled at the prospect of soaring tax rates in their communities if these cities and towns must absorb all Catholic-school pupils. So a fiscal crisis in Catholic parishes creates ripples felt throughout the local communities served by these schools.

As noted, this financial panic felt by non-Catholics has resulted in a dramatic turn-about on the question of granting public aid to nonpublic schools in America. A decade ago the question was so controversial that John Kennedy could probably not have encouraged such aid and gained the White House. And, as a matter of fact, Kennedy opposed aid to Catholic schools.

This preceded the ecumenical progress of the last ten years. Then, too, the cost factor wasn't so desperate. Catholic parents have always felt the strain of the double financial burden of carrying two school systems without financial relief. However, when the sixties opened, Catholic school enrollments were soaring, and the severe financial crisis of the seventies was not yet in sight.

As early as 1963, Gallup Poll reporters documented a shift in sentiment on aid to parochial schools.[9] In March, 1961, only 36 percent of persons interviewed said that federal aid should go to parochial and private schools, as well as public schools. By February, 1963, only two years later, 51 percent said that Catholic and private schools should receive federal aid. This change in attitude, therefore, began shifting even before the financial crisis hit schools, for in 1963 the Catholic school enrollment was still increasing.

A later poll conducted by Gallup indicated that more than 80 percent of those living in areas served by public, private and parochial schools would re-establish all three types of schools if they were to build new communities.

The most dramatic change in opinion concerning aid to Catholic schools involves the stand of Protestant and Jewish official organizations. In 1971 the Massachusetts Council of Churches, representing eleven denominations and 1,700 individual churches in the state, modified its stand against government aid to nonpublic schools by urging financial assistance. It stated: "Nonpublic schools that develop and submit creative and workable programs to improve the quality of educational opportunity for the poor, including strong parental involvement and cross-cultural appreciation, should be allocated funds by the state."

Even Billy Graham, the noted Protestant evangelist, said in 1971 that it seems wrong in principle "for people to be taxed to support a truly secular education (in public schools) while at the same time having to pay for educating their children in Church schools."[10] Graham called for "some creative solution to this complex (school) problem, perhaps through dual enrollment, tax rebates or tuition grants to students."

The American Jewish community has also seen a major reassessment of its position on government aid to religious schools. [11]

The new Jewish attitude is affected partially by the new ecumenical climate that has developed since the Vatican Council's historic declaration on the Jews; it also reflects a growing disenchantment with the public schools. In delivering his presidential address to the New York Board of Rabbis, Rabbi Harold I. Saperstein said: "I believe that the time has come for a re-evaluation of our position. There is a need for an intensified search for means by which a measure of aid can be given within the framework of our Constitution and without violating the principle of separation."

IS PUBLIC AID TO PRIVATE SCHOOLS POSSIBLE?

The question of financial aid to Catholic schools has always been a touchy one. Words charged with emotion have crept into the debate. One hears such phrases as: "There's a wall of separation between church and state in America"; "The Constitution forbids giving aid to any religious group"; or "Americans don't want to have an officially-sanctioned, or established church, such as England has."

A country like ours has been created and built by many different people, with varying cultural and religious backgrounds. Therefore, it is natural to be alarmed about the possibility that any one group would gain political or educational control and force its will on the rest of the country. We're used to deciding things on the basis of majority rule; anything else seems undemocratic.

A key concept is expressed by the word pluralism. This ideal is summarized in our motto: "from many, one." Such a goal is not easily accomplished, nor is it ever completely possible without some friction. And some commentators would remind us that a certain amount of polarization is healthy; some tension indicates growth and maturation.

Pluralism really means a respect for differences, yet a constant regard for the common good. Thomas Jefferson suggested that some coercion is sometimes necessary to produce uniformity. However, he added, complete uniformity of opinion is as undesirable as having everyone look exactly alike.

I am reminded of this delicate balance during most national elections. Very often the presidential winner receives only a slim majority of the votes cast. With the difference of a few percentage points, a man walks into the White House, yet 45 percent of the Americans who just voted may not even want him there. What is there for these Americans to do except grumble a little and hope for better results in the next presidential election? This is the price we pay for achieving unity while remaining individuals with differing opinions.

In recent years most Americans have longed for some good old-fashioned unity, while our society has been torn apart and polarized. Differing viewpoints have turned youth against those over thirty, and black against white. It has been a great challenge to get individuals with opposing opinions to listen calmly to one another and perhaps even discover a consensus.

Perhaps it is because we have recently agonized through all these other polarizations that the antagonism toward Catholic schools has decreased dramatically. There appears to be a new educational openness— the result of a desire for unity, and an understanding of the financial pressures exerted on public treasuries by private-school closings.

THE LEGAL QUESTION

The larger question legally is whether the United States Constitution permits the federal government to aid nonpublic schools.

A recent study by the National Catholic Educational Association, completed before the 1971 landmark Supreme Court decision, showed that many of the states which extend little or no aid to nonpublic schools, do not do so because they are prevented from offering such aid by their own state constitutions.[12] Then, when the Supreme Court ruled the Pennsylvania and Rhode Island aid formulas unconstitutional, many states felt that current legislative attempts to obtain state aid would have to be dropped.

As a matter of fact, even before the Supreme Court decision of June,1971, all kinds of aid had already been given to religious schools in America. As of May 15,1971, thirty-six states were extending some form of aid to their nonpublic schools. The other fourteen states gave nonpublic schools no assistance, though some private schools in those states were receiving federal aid.[13] New York state, for example, with 35.7 percent of the population Catholic, had eight different aid programs for nonpublic schools.

Such aid takes many forms: bus transportation, aid to disadvantaged students, health and welfare services, driver-education courses, shared-time programs, textbook loans, tax credits, leasing of nonpublic school facilities, and school lunch programs.

There are two sections of the United States Constitution that are significant in terms of aid to nonpublic schools. The First Amendment to the Constitution says "Congress shall make no law respecting an establishment of religion or prohibiting the free exercise thereof . . . ."

The Supreme Court has felt that the Fourteenth Amendment extends this guarantee to the states: " . . . no state shall make or enforce any law which shall abridge the privileges or immunities of citizens of the United States, nor shall any state deprive any person of life, liberty, or property without due process of law: nor deny to any person within its jurisdiction the equal protection of the laws. . . ."

These references, as you can see, do not speak specifically of aiding Catholic schools. And, of course, the men who drafted our Constitution couldn't have imagined that a vast Catholic school system would be born in America. Our colonial leaders, as well as those who later voted the above amendments did know that they didn't want an "established" religion here and they tried to prevent this by means of the above regulations.

Legally, this means that public schools can't face religious questions head-on, because the First and Fourteenth Amendments seem to forbid the federal and state governments from espousing any religion in the public schools or elsewhere. A dramatic figure of speech has appeared in aid-to-Catholic school discussions:"the wall of separation between church and state."

The United States Constitution does not refer to a wall separating church and state. The expression was first used in a letter written by President Thomas Jefferson in 1802 to the Baptist Association in Danbury, Connecticut. In 1879, the phrase appeared in a United States Supreme Court decision for the first time. The Jesuit, Neil McCluskey, has voiced the opinion that the only kind of American "wall" that makes sense is the stout affirmation that the Church will stay out of the state's business and the state out of religious affairs. And Robert Hutchins, an American educator, has said "the phrase 'wall of separation between church and state' has no future in America. What has a future is the rational, non-metaphorical discussion, in the light of all the provisions of the First Amendment, of the methods by which we may guarantee and promote religious freedom, and the methods by which we may bring about an educational system worthy of the potentialities and responsibilities of our people."[14]

Yet the metaphor persists, for most people—referring to the increased involvement of church and state in America—still speak of a "crumbling wall."[15]

THE UNITED STATES SUPREME COURT SPEAKS

The task of applying the constitutional test to legislation in America has been assigned to our courts. This is the system of "checks and balances" our government structure was designed to provide. With three branches of government, the executive (the Presidency), the legislative (Congress), and the judicial (the Supreme Court and lower courts), you are able to have such a balance with each branch acting as a brake upon the other two. We should note that the question of judicial review has been a troublesome one for constitutional scholars. Article III of the U.S. Constitution says "... the Supreme Court shall have appellate jurisdiction, ... *with such exceptions, and under such regulations as the Congress shall make."* (emphasis added)

It's quite obvious what effect the President and Congress have on our lives. Perhaps the Supreme Court's impact is not quite so direct and obvious. Yet, as the highest court in the land, it studies cases and the laws behind them, to guarantee that basic rights are not violated.

The Supreme Court, as the highest court of the United States, was established by Article III of the Constitution of the United States. The judicial power of the Court extends to all cases arising under the Constitution, laws and treaties of the United States, along with other cases. When the Court rules against the constitutionality of a statute or an executive action—as it did in its 1971 ruling on Catholic school aid—its decision can be overcome only if the Constitution is amended or the Court later overrules itself or modifies its opinion. Thus, the United States Supreme Court actually guides the development of American law.

However, lest we think that this procedure is, therefore, very tidy and black-and-white, we should be aware that there are all shades of gray involved here too. Most decisions by the Supreme Court are not unanimous ones. Thus, there is some difference of opinion among the justices when they hear and weigh the arguments of a case. Often when the decision is handed down, a minority report is also released. In this report, those justices who do not agree with the majority opinion have a chance to voice their own arguments. In some cases those filing a minority report do agree with the majority decision, but want to add their own special reasons.

Public reaction to Supreme Court rulings is also varied. Acceptance depends upon our moral agreement and inner consent, as well as our understanding of the reasoning behind the law. Thus, the law need not command our inner consent, only our outer obedience.

An interesting aspect of the Supreme Court rulings is the development of its doctrine. This concept applies to theology too. For example, in the years following the Vatican Council, many Catholics have had their religious equilibrium upset because things they were taught as truths in previous years no longer seem to be stressed in the liberal teaching of the Catholic Church.

These people were raised with one vision of the Church as a fixed, immutable religious form. Then they found that they were transported suddenly into a different vision of the Church with an emphasis upon openness and growth. The resulting confusion causes people to ask the basic question: "What should I believe?"

Theologians tried to dispel the confusion by explaining the development of doctrine—that most beliefs do not emerge full-blown and immutable for all ages. Rather, doctrine develops gradually, and with this evolving understanding comes a more complete definition of dogma. It's almost as if we had only a partial view of a belief, and with succeeding generations we will see it more completely (as our society becomes more enlightened and our tools of inquiry are sharpened). This development-of-doctrine concept is intimately linked to the continual attempt churches are making to speak to society in modern and relevant religious forms.

Applying this development-of-doctrine concept to the Supreme Court decisions, we can examine some of the confusion resulting from apparently contradictory decisions by the United States high court. Even its 1971 decision against purchase of secular services in Catholic schools, contradicts, in some ways, its previous trend.

It is also true that *some* Supreme Court justices are more conservative or liberal than others (often depending to some degree upon the outlook of the Presidents who appoint the justices to the Court). Supreme Court decisions will reflect the *current* court majority.

Affecting decisions also will be the changing social outlook. Some things considered radical in one decade will be quite easily accepted in the next. A well-known example is the battle waged by President Franklin D. Roosevelt against the Supreme Court. The Court showed a conservative mood with President Roosevelt in office originally. Congress then passed economic legislation of a far-reaching and novel character. Soon these new laws were attacked on constitutional grounds. From 1935 to 1937, the Supreme Court struck down major pieces of New Deal legislation. Gradually the liberals gained a slight majority in the Court. The Social Security Act was upheld in the Supreme Court by a mere five-to-four decision. With the economic changes within American society since that time, however, the legislation is considered quite mild today.

CHURCH-STATE COURT DECISIONS

In the church-state area, there has been a development of doctrine too, climaxed by the latest high-court ruling on aid to Catholic schools. In church-state decisions there are various aspects of changing opinion. One basic ingredient is the ecumenical spirit we have spoken of previously: a second, the experience of having had a Catholic President. Both factors have helped calm some anxiety Americans felt about Catholic power. A third factor has been the broadening concept of "welfare" reflected in society and in the Supreme Court cases. Federal legislation, such as the Economic Opportunity Act and the Elementary and Secondary Education

Act of 1965, have provided some aid to Catholic schools; thus the climate in Congress has been changing too.

Two recent Supreme Court decisions provided the background for the latest court ruling on aid to nonpublic schools. In 1963, the Supreme Court banned relgious practices in public schools (thus, "shaking up" many Americans who felt alarm at the removal of religion from America's schools). And, in the Allen decision, in 1968, the Court approved providing textbooks for Catholic schools.

The landmark decisions of 1971 (*Lemon and DiCenso*) ruled that if the government paid salaries for teachers of secular subjects in religious schools, it was involved in "excessive entanglement" with religion. We will look very closely at that decision and its ramifications. First, however, we should trace the highlights in the developing doctrine of church and state in America, as reflected in Supreme Court decisions. (After each decision listed below, is given the volume and page reference from *United States Reports, Cases Adjudged in the Supreme Court*.)[16]

1908 *Quick Bear v. Leupp*, 210 U.S. (1908)
". . . We cannot concede the proposition that Indians cannot be allowed to use their own money to educate their own children in the schools of their own choice because the government is necessarily undenominational."

1925 *Pierce et.al.v. Society of Sisters*, 268 U.S. 510 (1925)
Here the court denied that a state can require children to attend public schools only. ". . . The fundamental theory of liberty upon which all governments in this union repose excludes any general power of the state to standardize its children by forcing them to accept instruction from public teachers only. The child is not the mere creature of the State"; The Supreme Court thereby affirmed the importance of educational diversity in America—based on parental and educational rights.

1930 *Cochranv. Louisiana State Board of Education*, 0 281 U.S. 370 (1930)
The Supreme Court here unanimously upheld a decision permitting the use of state-owned textbooks by pupils attending Catholic schools because "the school children and the state alone are the beneficiaries."

1947 *Everson v. Board of Education*, 330 U.S. 1 (1947)
The Court declared that New Jersey's provision of bus

transportation for Catholic school pupils was legal. This decision gave recognition to the principle that pupils in non-public schools can be included in the programs of "general welfare" for children.

1948 *McCollum v. Board of Education*, 333 U.S. 203 (1948)
This decision prohibited "released time" for religious instruction by various denominations on school property during school hours.

1954 *Zorach v. Clauson*, 343 U.S. 306 (1952)
Here the Court allowed "dismissed time" for the religious instruction of public school children given off public-school premises.

1960 *Shelton v. Tucker*, 364 U.S. 479 (1960)
The Court, in this case, proclaimed: "The vigilant protection of constitutional freedoms is nowhere more vital than in the community of American schools."

1963 *School District of Abington Township, Pennsylvania, et. al. v. Schempp, et. al.*, 374 U.S. 302, 222 (1963)
In this case the Court ruled that Bible reading and recitation of the Lord's Prayer in public schools, with voluntary participation by students, are unconstitutional on the ground that they violate the Establishment of Religion Clause of the First Amendment. Here the justices issued a new test: "What are the purpose and the primary effect of the enactment? If either is the advancement or inhibition of religion then the enactment exceeds the scope of legislative power as circumscribed by the Constitution."

1968 *Board of Education v. Allen*, 392 U.S. 236 (1968)
In this decision, the Court declared constitutional the New York law requiring local school boards to purchase books with state funds and lend them to Catholic-school students. Here, too, the Court stated that religious-related schools "play a significant and valuable role in raising national levels of knowledge, competence and experience." The justices added:"... the continued willingness to rely on private school systems, including parochial systems, strongly suggests that a wide segment of informed opinion legislative and otherwise, has found that these schools do an acceptable job of providing secular education to their students. This judgment is further evidence that parochial schools are performing, in addition to their sectarian function, the task of secular education."

1970   *Walz v. Tax Commission*, 397 U.S. 664 (1970)
The Court here concluded that the legislative purpose of
the New York property tax exemption constituted
"neither the advancement nor the inhibition of religion." The
Court majority affirmed that houses of religious worship are
"beneficial and stabilizing influences in community life." The
Chief Justice, writing for the majority, defined "Establishment
of Religion" as understood by the framers of the First
Amendment, to connote "sponsorship, financial support and
active involvement of the sovereign in religious activity."

THE SUPREME COURT ISSUES NEW GUIDELINES

In the light of the Walz determination and the 1971 Supreme Court decision, a new phrase has probably taken the forefront as the pivotal key in
church-state relationships. The concept of a "wall of separation" has now
been conceived in terms of *excessive entanglement*. This phrase— and the
realities it represents—now serve as a new guideline for consideration of
aid to Catholic schools.

As we entered the decade of the seventies, the United States
Supreme Court agreed to hear argument in several key school-aid cases.
Excitement was in the air that this would in all likelihood be a landmark
decision, as in fact it turned out.

On June 28, 1971, the United States Supreme Court released its decisions in three significant cases: *Lemon*, *DiCenso*, and *Tilton*.

The Tilton case concerned aid to sectarian colleges in Connecticut.
Here church-related higher education won a 5-4 decision which declared
constitutional the use of federal funds to construct buildings on campuses
of church-related colleges and universities, provided no religious use is
made of said buildings. (The Higher Education Facilities Act of 1963 ex-
pressly excludes "any facility used or to be used for sectarian instruction
or as a place for religious worship, or . . . any facility which . . . is used or to
be used primarily in connection with any part of the program of a school
or department of divinity . . . .)

The remaining two cases, however, directly relate to Catholic elementary and secondary schools. These cases will be considered at length
here.

Rhode Island's 1969 Salary Supplement Act provided for ⸜ 15 percent salary supplement to be paid to teachers in nonpublic schools, at
which the average per-pupil expenditure on secular education is below
the average in public schools. Eligible teachers must teach only courses
offered in the public schools, and must agree not to teach courses in
religion.

Pennsylvania's Nonpublic Elementary and Secondary Education Act, passed in 1968, authorized the state Superintendent of Public Instruction to "purchase" certain "secular educational services" from nonpublic schools, directly reimbursing those schools solely for teachers' salaries, textbooks, and instructional materials. Reimbursement was restricted to courses in specific secular subjects.

The complaint challenging the constitutionality of such programs alleged that the church-affiliated schools are controlled by religious organizations, have the purpose of propagating and promoting a particular religious faith, and conduct their operations to fulfill that purpose.

The Court held that both statutes are unconstitutional under the Religion Clause of the First Amendment, as the cumulative impact of the entire relationship arising under the statutes involves excessive entanglement between government and religion. The Court referred to three basic tests that ought to be applied to such laws. "First, the statute must have a secular legislative purpose; second, its principal or primary effect must be one that neither advances nor inhibits religion, . . . finally, the statute must not foster 'an excessive government entanglement with religion' ".

The key concept in the Court's consideration is that of excessive entanglement. The justices felt that entanglement in the Rhode Island program arises because of the religious activity and purpose of the church-affiliated schools, especially with respect to children of impressionable age in the primary grades, and the dangers that a teacher under religious control and discipline poses to the separation of religious from purely secular aspects of elementary education in such schools. They added that the entanglement in the Pennsylvania program also arises from the restrictions and surveillance necessary to ensure that teachers play a strictly nonideological role.

The Court spoke frankly about the difficulty of determining where the line should be drawn on church-state relationships. "Candor compels acknowledgment, . . . that we can only dimly perceive the lines of demarcation in this extraordinarily sensitive area of constitutional law."

The new decision seems to bury the image of a wall of separation. "Our prior holdings do not call for total separation between church and state; total separation is not possible in an absolute sense. Some relationship between government and religious organizations is inevitable." And "Judicial caveats against entanglement must recognize that the line of separation, far from being a 'wall', is a blurred, indistinct and variable barrier depending on all the circumstances of a particular relationship."

The Court closely examined whether it is, indeed, possible for Catholic-school teachers to be exclusively secular. Two documents submitted to scrutiny were the Rhode Island Diocesan *Handbook of School Regulations* and Rev. Joseph Fichter's sociological study of a parochial school which asserts that religion permeates the curriculum and atmosphere of a

Catholic school. The *Handbook* states that "Religious formation is not confined to formal courses; nor is it restricted to a single subject area."

Another aspect of the cases that caused the justices concern was the divisive political potential. "A broader base of entanglement of yet a different character is presented by the divisive political potential of these state programs. Ordinarily political debate and division, however vigorous or even partisan, are normal and healthy manifestations of our democratic system of government, but political division along religious lines was one of the principal evils against which the First Amendment was intended to protect."

In the text of these cases, as in previous cases, the United States Supreme Court had high praise for the work of the Catholic schools in America. ". . . Nothing we have said can be construed to disparage the role of church-related elementary and secondary schools in our national life. Their contribution has been and is enormous. Nor do we ignore their economic plight in a period of rising costs and expanding need. Taxpayers generally have been spared vast sums by the maintenance of these educational institutions by religious organizations, largely by the gifts of faithful adherents."

Catholic schools didn't just need praise, however; they needed financial support. Has support been ruled out completely by this 1971 decision?

Many Catholic educators were, quite literally, stunned by the decision. The trend of the Court seemed, up to this point, to be moving toward more cooperation between church and state. The Court seemed to feel there were ways of dealing with separation without severely penalizing private institutions.

Catholic educational leaders also knew that public opinion was changing dramatically and that most Americans were in favor of such aid. It seemed to many Catholic educators, therefore, that relief was right around the corner. The Court decision does not reflect public opinion, necessarily; instead it must be concerned with legal analysis. Ironically, however, one argument the Court used was that the legislative battles would stir up public controversy. The Court ignored completely the polls indicating that most Americans would prefer aid to Catholic schools at the present time, and, thus, argument on the subject would probably not be as heated as the Court predicted.

When the decision was announced the Supreme Court statement was strengthened by the fact that it was almost a unanimous decision. Clearly the Court at this time will not permit direct aid to private schools in the form of salaries.

There are other possibilities, however, and Catholic educators are now considering them. Rev. C. Albert Koob, president of the National Catholic Educational Association, said: "This is not the end of Catholic education. It tells us the perimeters in which we've got to work and sends us back to the drawing boards to find some other means that avoids the entanglement with religion which the Court found unconstitutional."

One possibility is to consider programs that offer aid to students or parents instead of schools, such as scholarship grants or tax credits.

Charles M. Whelan, S.J., professor of law at Fordham Law School, says: "So far as tuition payments and voucher plans are concerned, care will have to be taken not to incorporate into the programs the same secular-religious distinctions and policing that proved fatal to the Pennsylvania and Rhode Island statutes."

An interesting analysis of these Supreme Court decisions appears in the report of President Nixon's Panel on Nonpublic Education. "In the Panel's view the full Court had an inadequate perception of realities in parochial schools because it failed to pierce the institutional veil. The entire focus was on the powers of the hierarchy, the role of the pastors, and the teaching commitment of religious; ignored were parents, teachers, and pupils who are now cut off from certain forms of public assistance."

The Panel's report adds: " . . . It might be noted that some constitutional lawyers feel the time has come to challenge the denial of benefits to nonpublic school students on grounds that educational appropriations are public welfare benefits which should not be restricted by religious conditions. The challenge should be mounted."

Faced with the June, 1971 Supreme Court decision, and the threatened extinction of nonpublic schools in America, several concepts are developing.

Subsequent court cases (outside of the United States Supreme Court) have dealt with attempts to provide monetary aid to nonpublic schools. Pennsylvania initiated a system of grants to parents of children in nonpublic schools. However, this was viewed unfavorably by federal judges. Three federal circuit judges also ruled unconstitutional Ohio's parent reimbursement grant program of up to $90 per year for tuition paid for their children. A three-judge federal panel in New York City ruled part of the 1972 state aid law unconstitutional.

William C. McInnes, S. J. the president of Fairfield University (the institution involved in the Supreme Court's *Tilton* case), issued a warning in *America* magazine: "In my opinion, it would be a grave mistake to look exclusively to the courts as the determinant of the place of church-related education in this country's life. It is school leaders, as well as lawyers, who should play a leading role in the flow of history and the evolution of constitutional insight into church-related educational systems." (September 18, 1971)

As a result of the June, 1971 Supreme Court decisions, more than forty suits bearing on the constitutionality of aid to church-related schools began working their way through the lower federal and state courts. In the meantime, the presentation of the justice of aid to nonpublic schools has been more effectively voiced since the June, 1971 setback. These arguments were summarized by Brother Francis Huether, FSC, in a memo sent out to members of his community:

Public good and public policy must transcend rigid, negative constitutionalism; individual and minority rights must be protected also against a monolithic educational establishment.

Since state financing is inevitable, it ought to be used at once to preserve alternatives to public schools.

Moral and ethical values are essential to education.

Equity, freedom, fairness, and cultural diversity demand pluralism of school systems.

All these arguments reflect a renewed emphasis on educational pluralism and parental rights.

The most significant result of the June, 1971 Supreme Court decisions was the organization of a national effort to develop and legislate a concept known as *tax credit.*

There will be more litigation ahead in the area of aid to Catholic schools. Catholic parents hope to be able to find a formula to give them some financial relief. And non-Catholic taxpayers continue to be nervous about the financial impact of Catholic-school closings.

The crucial impact of the decision could be found in the number of school closings as a direct result of having the door closed so emphatically on direct aid. No panic reaction resulted. The National Catholic Educational Association estimated that about 8 percent of existing schools would close in the light of the decision. This involves about 800 schools, roughly 400 more than were expected to close whatever the Court decided.

Some Catholics are breathing a sigh of relief that the sacred-secular division now appears unnecessary in Catholic schools. Many teachers would have found it difficult to honor such a division and would have felt that this was a high price to pay for public aid. Now, perhaps, new ways can be devised that do not require that Catholic teachers nervously worry about whether certain teaching would be permitted. Catholic schools are thus freed to be totally committed religious witnesses to their local communities.

In the meantime, the Catholic Church now faces unprecedented pressure to establish and expand sensible management procedures. It may be that one hard-to-see-but-happy result of the decision could be that the Church will now be forced to restructure its system creatively. Out of these dark days may come some of the finest educational leadership— simply because there are no options now except to abdicate completely or be absolutely brilliant!

CATHOLIC SCHOOLS WITHOUT FEDERAL AID

You may recall that in the days of the Baltimore Councils, it was a zealous layman, James A. McMaster, who spurred American bishops into expanding the fledgling Catholic-school system into a national movement to build a parish school next to every Catholic church.

Once again the American church has been challenged by a Catholic layman who presents these two dramatic theses:

1. American Catholics should still work realistically toward the goal of every Catholic student in a Catholic school, and
2. American Catholics can and should pay the bills for such an expanded system themselves, and not get involved in the search for public aid.

It is a refreshing proposal, and after you catch your breath at the apparent unrealistic daring of the challenge, you must, in fairness, listen to this lawyer's case.

William E. Brown, a Wisconsin attorney, learned his money-management techniques in the best school possible—American industry. He has served, since 1932, in the Legal Department of the Allis-Chalmers Manufacturing Company; he evidently would like to see the same sound management techniques employed by the Catholic Church in the financial adminstration of her school system.

Brown recently co-authored a book with Andrew M. Greeley, of the Greeley-Rossi research team. The volume, entitled *Can Catholic Schools Survive?* contains his financial plan of action discussed here.[17]

Brown's basic tenets are quite simple.

When Catholics pay tuition to attend Catholic schools, it is not considered a tax-deductible expense. However, Brown notes that Catholics do receive a 20 percent deduction on their income tax for all religious contributions. Therefore, if the Church really pushed for more contributions, and did away with Catholic school tuition completely, all Catholic contributors would, in effect, receive a "gift" from the federal government—a 20 percent income tax savings. Brown strongly recommends that Catholic schools completely drop tuition payments. It would be interesting to see how—and if—this could work in practice.

As a matter of fact, though, Catholics would not get 20 percent off on their income tax, or 20 percent savings on their tax bill. Even the 20 percent is just an average, but you get it on the taxes you would have paid *on the part of your income* you give to your religious group.

Brown's second thesis is just as straightforward. He says Catholics must realize that every time a Catholic school closes, and pupils must be absorbed by the local public school, Catholics themselves are paying the bill for this higher public-school cost. In fact, a large percentage of Catholic schools in America are located in major urban centers. In these urban areas, there is also a higher percentage of Catholics in the general population. When the local taxes jump because of the influx of pupils from closing Catholic schools, most of the taxpayers are Catholic, and they are ending up paying the bill anyway. It might be cheaper, Brown argues, for Catholics to increase their tax-deductible church donations than to pay increased taxes. Again, other factors should be considered here. School taxes have, in the past, been raised largely from property owners. Even in cities, most property owners are not Catholics. Thus, Catholics may not be paying a higher percentage of the educational costs. The educational cost base could shift to federal or state aid under pressure from court rulings that educational inequalities based on property taxes are unconstitutional. However, since Catholics are not proportionately wealthy, even under the new system, probably Catholics would not carry most of the urban educational costs, as Brown notes.

Brown says there are several distinct disadvantages to Catholics themselves if public aid is received. Without public funding, there is an intense pressure placed on Catholic schools to improve in order to compete effectively for students, in spite of the high costs. If Catholics gain public financial support, some of this pressure for improvement would ease. He notes also that this financial aid from the public sector is derived from taxes paid by the American people, including many Catholics. Catholics now constitute 23.5 percent of America's total population. So Catholics are helping to pay the bill either way—with donations or with their own tax money.

In addition, Brown calls us a "whimpering generation" when it come to complaining about the high costs of Catholic schools today. His figures seem to indicate that, despite increased costs, our generation is actually able to support Catholic schools more easily than our forefathers did. He compares taxes, inflation, wages, etc., for the past, the present, and the predicted future, to reach that conclusion.

Brown has made some radical charges. Does he substantiate them?

American Church leaders cannot afford to seek solutions to existing school problems without analyzing Brown's facts and figures. There are some thought-provoking concepts to be digested by all those who see federal funding as a panacea.

There are some flaws in his presentation, however,

While his financial data are documented and he thoroughly grasps management practices, Brown tends to make glaring generalizations occasionally that are contradicted by the facts. In a few instances, as one analyst has commented, he is embarrassingly careless with factual references.[18]

And Brown limits himself to a "black-or white" argument; he considers only the case of Catholic schools as they are tremendously expanded (with every Catholic child in a Catholic school), or simply having no Catholic schools. He thereby eliminates all possibilities in between— more cooperative efforts between Catholics and public schools, other types of Catholic schools(like Christian Education Centers, etc.).

Brown notes that only a small percentage of education funding comes from the federal source at the present time. And he uses this fact to show that federal aid wouldn't benefit Catholics that much. But he ignores a fact he must be aware of: that, if constitutional avenues can be found, the trend in the future could include a much larger slice of educational funding with federal dollars. This destroys some of the power of his columns of figures.

Brown's management advice to bishops and school administratros would greatly improve the efficiency of the Church's educational program, no matter what shape it takes in the future. His zeal in providing Catholic education for all Catholic children is admirable, as McMaster's was.

There are some loopholes in his arguments, but his facts should be studied as we seek solutions to current educational problems in the Church. However, even with his powerful statistics, it may be unrealistic to expect that Catholics could and would continue to support Catholic schools without some kind of assistance.

Some schools *are* demonstrating remarkable self-help. Boston College recently noted that Carnegie Foundation studies indicate that private colleges will not survive without aid. At the same time, however, the university announced that through discipline and economic responsibility, BC balances its budget in fiscal 1971-72. The school thus began operating in a brand new economic context.

ANOTHER CHOICE—THE VOUCHER PLAN

Another radical financial plan for American education has been proposed and has stirred a certain amount of controversy. The concept is one of the most revolutionary to hit school administrators in many decades. It is based upon a piece of paper called a voucher.

The voucher plan was proposed by University of Chicago economist Milton Friedman in 1953. It has been most completely analyzed by the Center for the Study of Public Policy in Cambridge, Massachusetts.[19] Details of the plan, summarized here, are taken from that document and from releases issued by that organization.

Voucher experimentation and evaluation are currently underway. This type of scrutiny is vital to new educational ideas. The Office of Economic Opportunity (OEO) is currently sponsoring a research analysis. And the United States Office of Education will watch the results closely. This analytical approach is sound, since the only sensible way to evaluate such a program is to try it and see what happens.

The basic idea is relatively simple. A local educational voucher agency (EVA) would issued a voucher to parents. The parents would take the voucher to the public or private school of their choice. The school would return the voucher to the EVA, which in turn would send the school a check equal to the value of the voucher. As a result, public subsidies for education would go only to schools in which parents chose to enroll their children.

Actually, the GI Bill provided a type of voucher, allowing veterans to select higher education from the college of their choice.

The United States Supreme Court will probably rule on the voucher's constitutionality. The Court could indicate, however, that the GI Bill concept is acceptable because college-level students are involved. The 1971 Supreme Court aid decisions indicated that something acceptable for colleges (like *Tilton*) won't be acceptable at the elementary and secondary level. Therefore, many experts fear the voucher plan is not feasible constitutionally.

The educational arguments for the voucher plan rest on three assumptions. The first is that the voucher scheme would lead to a greater diversity of educational alternatives. Secondly, poor parents, given financial resources and insured equitable admissions treatment, would be able to exercise greater choice among the alternatives. Thus, the schools would have to be more responsive to their children's needs. This should result in parents' having greater control over the education of their children. Thirdly, the diversity of educational alternatives and the increased responsiveness of schools to children's needs would lead to improved education, particularly for poor children. It could also be true, however, that poor parents would be more prone to fall for the easy and flashily-promoted education.

There are three important ground rules added to the basic voucher system. No voucher school should be able to charge parents tuition in addition to the voucher amount. This would prevent discrimination against the children of poor families who could not afford such extra tuition charges. In addition, in order to give all students an unbiased chance for admission to schools of their choice, participating schools with more places than applicants would enroll all applicants. Schools with more applicants than places would accept a portion of their students, say half, by their own criteria and the other half at random. Thirdly, all participating schools should provide parents with enough information concerning educational programs to permit parents to make an informed choice among schools for their children.

Christopher Jencks, director of the Center for the Study of Public Policy, says that the main argument in favor of the voucher plan is that public schools are not responsive today because they are monopolies; they have no competition. There simply is no other place for most urban children to go to learn how to function well in society. Jencks feels that steps to insure integration could easily be guaranteed by the plan. Those who favor the plan feel that giving parents more control over their children's education is a valuable asset of the plan. Parents are then in a position to demand accountability from the schools they support. This would be especially valuable for urban poor families.

There have been potential criticisms of the plan, however. Civil rights organizations warn that—without strong protection—the voucher could be used to avoid integration and to channel funds into select private schools. They are afraid, in other words, that the voucher plan would perpetuate segregation. The National Education Association, and other teachers' groups, feel strongly that vouchers would weaken, or perhaps destroy, the public-school system in America.

Voucher-plan experiments should show whether these potential troubles will indeed arise in the actual operation of the plan.

Certainly one of the major problems of the voucher is the possibility that schools in America will be segregated, based on economic need. Theodore R. Sizer, Dean of Harvard's Graduate School of Education, has helped develop a unique voucher proposal that would directly aid the poor. Called the "Poor Children's Bill of Rights" and patterned after the GI Bill, this plan will frankly discriminate in favor of the poor and culturally disadvantaged. "In the simplest scheme, all children defined as poor would receive a grant of $1500 per year, or more than twice the current per-pupil national expenditure. In more sophisticated schemes, the poorer the child, the more valuable the certificate, the assumption being that a child from a severely constricted background will require and deserve more expensive services than children who are better off. What is important is that the size of the grant be large enough to make a significant pedagogical difference and that it be large enough to be seen as desirable by middle-class schools."[20] Some commentators have warned that the voucher plan does not have enough grassroots support. This may prove its undoing.

One of the greatest advantages of such a plan is that by creating competition between schools, public and private, the Poor Children's Bill of Rights will promote the establishment of new schools, responsive to the communities they serve, particularly in black, urban areas. (This concept is quite similar to the basic premise for the establishment of a separate school system in America by the Catholic Church a century ago.)

If the Catholic-school system participates— even indirectly—in an abandonment of inner city poor, it will be a drastic desertion of what should be one of the chief apostolates of the Church in America.

Without the voucher, Catholic schools face the criticism of catering only to those who can pay. Educators can, quite justly, reply that in order to remain open they must charge high tuitions; nevertheless, high tuition bills are preventing many inner-city youth from receiving compensatory education. The Church should aid in providing such educational service for the poor.

Catholic schools in America were born to serve the immigrant poor and their special needs. If they now become affiliated mainly with those who can pay, a potentially dangerous situation exists because of the alliance of the Church with the wealthy. This union causes serious repercussions (as it has in Europe, the anticlericalism of the French Revolution being only one example). And it could cause revolutions in the developing nations in the next few decades. In America, the Church cannot desert the poor without risking a real credibility gap, as the result of preaching one thing and doing another.

It's true that the Church's educational mission is not exclusively for the poor. Catholics in suburban areas can have their own brand of spiritual poverty. However, it would be the worst kind of reversal of priorities to ignore the social dynamite existing in our urban areas.

TAX CREDIT

President Nixon's Panel on Nonpublic Education made quite a startling statement in its final report: "... [in 1976] when [our] nation celebrates its two-hundredth anniversary of independence, the fate of nonpublic schools, as they are known today, will have been largely determined."

The sense of urgency permeating that statement is also reflected in the rapid development of a fiscal and political reality—that of the tax credit. Little known before 1972, this topic was discussed heatedly around the country. The focal point was our nation's capital, for tax credit was endorsed by the President's finance commission studies, and countless bills were sent to the 92nd Congress providing for parental tax credits. The bill submitted by House Ways and Means Committee Chairman, Wilbur Mills, received the most attention, however, This was "a bill to amend the Internal Revenue Code of 1954 to allow a credit against the individual income tax for tuition paid for the elementary or secondary education of dependents."

The various bills in Congress differed in details but followed the same basic pattern. In general, a tax credit law would allow a parent who sends his children to nonpublic schools to subtract half of his tuition costs up to a maximum of $400 per child from his federal income tax. The amount of the tax credit would be reduced as the parent's income rose above a certain level.

A tax credit is far more valuable than the usual tax deduction. Unlike a deduction, it is worth its full "face value." A credit differs from a deduction in that deductions are subtracted before calculating one's income tax. Credits are subtracted from the sum due after the calculation is made. Supporters note that this does not involve a government grant because the government does not give the taxpayer anything. He simply reduces his tax by a specified amount.

Organized support for tax credit was led by a group called Citizens Relief for Education by Income Tax (CREDIT). CREDIT officers reflected membership support from Jewish groups, the Lutheran Church-Missouri Synod, the National Association of Independent Schools, along with the National Catholic Education Association, the National Union of Christian Schools, and the United States Catholic Conference. These combined constituencies total approximately five million children in schools operated under Protestant, Catholic, Jewish, and private auspices.

The tax credit approach also received endorsement in the report of the President's Panel on Nonpublic Education. The panel expressed confidence that tax credit legislation could meet constitutional criteria, promote the public good, elicit public support, and bolster the morale of parents of nonpublic school children.

The panel noted that a satisfactory tax credit statute would include compliance with federal civil rights requirements, limitation of tax credits to a fixed percentage of the tuition, a maximum tax credit per child, and a reduction in credit for high-income families.

As the CREDIT organizational brochures indicate, tax credits are not really new. They have been used for purposes other than education for many years. Retired taxpayers are the most common beneficiaries of tax credits. Some of the expense businesses run into for expansion of facilities can be credited against their taxes.

Several advantages can be cited for the tax credit approach. In the light of constitutional tests, it is advantageous that there is no direct transfer of funds from a public source to a religious school. The tax credit goes to the citizen—like other tax benefits for charity, medical expenses, etc.

Dr. Roger A. Freeman, Senior Fellow at Stanford University, has strongly recommended federal income tax credits as a means of preserving diversity and competition in American education. He cites the following advantages: many schools may be forced out of existence during the 1970s unless some type of action is taken to keep them alive; and tuition tax credits can help parents to augment their support of nonpublic schools without placing a commensurate burden on them.

One glaring disadvantage is that the tax credit approach does not help very poor parents of nonpublic school students who pay no income tax and, therefore, would receive no credit. While this is so, advocates note that assistance is already available through the Elementary and Secondary Education Act. Catholics and other nonpublic school personnel would have to struggle to avoid becoming "elitist" with tax credit funds. Most schools have subsidized the education of large numbers of low-income students for many years; this will clearly have to continue if these schools wish to avoid the elitist tag.

For middle income families a tax credit disadvantage is that fairly small amounts of money might be allotted to the individual, and contrasted with the voucher plan, this tax relief reaches only a small percentage of people.

Voucher plan supporters will cite a further disadvantage of tax credit—the fact that this plan seems to be in competition with voucher principles.

Some observers, warning that a tax credit bill could not get through Congress, urged that public school monies also be a part of tax credit legislation. While President Nixon promised property tax relief and equalization of school finances, the administration's top priority seemed to be basic fiscal reform. Tax credit could get lost in the shuffle of that reform.

The tax credit road leads almost inevitably to the courthouse. Tax credit supporters got encouragement on the judicial front when a Minnesota district court upheld that state's 1971 law giving tax credits to non-public school parents. This ruling was the first to sustain the constitutionality of such legislation.

In New York, a federal court test issued an opinion favorable to advocates of tax credit when the court refused to grant an injunction against a tax credit measure. An extremely helpful analysis of tax credit and constitutional law appeared in *America* magazine (October 14, 1972). Roy Lechtreck argues that "tax laws cannot support activities the states are not allowed to permit. But tax laws can support activities the government simply must not promote—for here the basic difference is that the initiative resides in the people, not the government."

Lechtreck says Senator Abraham A. Ribicoff has answered the argument that tax credits are unfair to the poor. "If this is a criticism, it applies with equal force to every deduction and credit now allowed by the Internal Revenue Code . . . . The man too poor to pay his hospital bill gets no benefit from the medical deduction available to his neighbor who does pay the bill. This proves that we need to help those who cannot pay their hospital bills; it does not prove that we should deny tax relief to those who pay these costs."

As the organization CREDIT points out, the exercise of the traditional right of choice is now outside the financial ability of many families. Educational choice should not be exclusively a function of wealth.

REDESIGNING CATHOLIC EDUCATION

We mentioned earlier that the two extreme positions concerning Catholic schools are "keep them as they are" or "close them all."

Neither viewpoint seems realistic or practical. But if this large structure must be overhauled in order to remain relevant, where do you begin?

You begin with money, and we've traveled that road. Now we must go down that other avenue leading to innovative design for Catholic education. Delineating specific changes to help Catholic education move forward in the demanding decades that lie ahead— that's the challenge. In some instances, this will mean creating drastically new designs for Catholic education. In other areas, it will involve taking the basic structure as it now stands and altering it somewhat. These alterations affect several different aspects of the Catholic-school system and we shall explore each one. Here is a brief summary of the four major areas. Then we shall explore each in greater depth.

ADMINISTRATIVE CHANGES—Who runs the schools? The Catholic-school management-structure is badly in need of renovation and repair. In general, the administration of Catholic schools must be more professional with an effective Board of Education at the helm. Such a board would involve parents and other lay people to a much greater degree. The laity in America must be forced into more educational leadership if the Church's educational program is to survive.

Another major feature of Catholic-school administration will be its regional organizational pattern. The local Catholic school— supported by only one parish—will probably disappear. All parochial schools may not necessarily close, but schools will no longer be confined to a single parish for support or for students.

Along with consolidation should be a pattern that can best be described by the word integration. Catholic-school programs must become more integrated with public-school operations. And within the Church itself, there must be more coordination between various educational programs: Catholic schools, Confraternity of Christian Doctrine, educational programs for youth and adults, Newman work on college campuses, etc. The Church can no longer afford the luxury of each department operating on its own without an organized, integrated effort.

CURRICULUM CHANGES—What do you teach? What your children study in school will be affected by the world in which they live. Dramatically changing times require changes in subject matter and approaches to teaching. Catholic schools face this dilemma specifically in teaching religion. Daring—and sometimes shocking—religious teaching methods will be employed in an attempt to make values and religious convictions relevant to modern society. As modern science (test-tube babies and interplanetary flight, for example) brings new theological problems, these dilemmas will create repercussions in classrooms.

Catholic schools must also face the question of whether they should be teaching math and science, or remain only with humane studies. And the biggest curriculum challenge of all will be in the area of communications. Too often, educators have "a message" but they are unable to communicate it to others.

TECHNOLOGICAL CHANGES—What equipment do you need? Educators refer to technology as "the hardware." The high priest of the movement is Marshall McLuhan. Opportunities here will be dramatic as new equipment becomes available, ranging from communications cassettes to computerized teaching-machines of all kinds.

One of the major developments will be the extension of the classroom via technology. *Sesame Street* television broadcasts have shown that media can turn a living room into a classroom. As more portable equipment becomes available, youth and adults will be able to absorb learning anywhere, much as they do now with paperback books. Because of the rapid developments in this area, one must develop a mind-set to get ready for the changes, even if one can't predict what each of the changes will be.

ARCHITECTURAL CHANGES—How do you utilize your buildings? One of the most serious challenges facing the Church today is the need to figure out what to do with all the buildings we've erected during our expansion phase. The entire physical plant of Catholic education needs retooling. In many cases this will involve finding new roles for existing structures; in some instances, it will require designing new structures. The basic question of what a church edifice should be has been raised recently. Spending large amounts of money on big churches might actually prevent a feeling of close community in congregations. New urban designs will force more practical utilization of space. As large new housing developments grow, schools and churches will be integrated into the over-all structure in new ways.

Within these four areas lie most of the forward thrusts Catholic education must make in order to achieve new insights and heights of excellence. This is the only way to create a system that will remain worthy of the sacrifices countless millions of individuals made to give this structure the life it has today. With the opportunity to incorporate sound new approaches, the vigor of Catholic education can grow; without this fresh blood flowing through its veins, Catholic educational development will be stunted, and the system could virtually die.

There isn't much time left.

BASIC CHANGE FACTORS

There are several aspects of educational change affecting all four structural areas listed above.

The first, simple nostalgia, can often be an obstacle to educational change. Some of this emotion stalls necessary educational changes in Catholic schools. Almost all of us are slightly unnerved by change: We tend to be creatures of habit; we usually prefer comfortable habits. Being jarred out of these habits (especially habits of thought) creates an uncomfortable sensation. Although all people are somewhat alarmed by change, it is unrealistic and impractical to fight all change.

You probably have experienced returning to a special place you remember fondly—maybe the neighborhood where you grew up, perhaps a country scene to which you were especially drawn. What often happens when you return? You discover that the old neighborhood has changed drastically, or a new skyscraper mars the beauty of your idyllic pastoral spot. Although this is sad, what can be done about it? Everyone favors sensible conservation. Sensible ecological principles must begin to balance man's idea of progress. Once these factors have been reasonably considered, however, progress cannot stand still simply to provide us with a good feeling when we return to our favorite locales.

To a degree, the same truth applies to educational change.

For most people, looking back on their school days evokes happy memories. Of course, the anxiety and uncertainty of adolescence presented some painful moments for most individuals as they passed through this time of life. However, if you were a good student you probably enjoyed school and did well there. Even if you were not a good student, when you think back, you remember the happy times for you: the basketball games, the school dances, or your graduation.

We leave school behind us, and then a happy haze develops around these memories as the years pass. We forget about bad teachers and the homework; we remember that we had relatively few problems and responsibilities then, and we like those "good old days."

When our children start school, it brings back the memories of our own school days. However, many years have passed and there are changes. We usually grow uncomfortable about these changes; we might even resent or reject them.

For example, the new math is unsettling to many parents because their education did not include this approach. These parents do want good educational experiences for their children. But always in the background is the parental memory of the time when they were students. It's impossible for the parents not to make comparisons; therefore, it's difficult for them not to be nostalgic and, thus, uneasy about educational changes.

Change presents a different problem for teachers and educational administrators. People in charge of schools are professionals. A substantial part of their job is to keep informed about new educational approaches, and to evaluate them. Among teachers and administrators you have variety too. So some educators dynamically push for change in schools while others aggressively oppose innovative ideas.

One commentator reminds us, however, that "the Church is, essentially, not an instrument for the preservation of the status quo, but rather a dynamic agent for bringing about change."[21]

A second facet of our Catholic-school innovation is closely related to change. This is the temptation of the educational fad. Fads come and go in education, just as they do in other fields.

Fads can be just as exciting in education as they are in clothing—and they can be just as short-lived. Most women didn't throw out a whole closet-full of clothing when the mini-skirt appeared. More likely, they held onto their "basic" outfits and made some adjustments in their hemlines so they didn't appear old-fashioned. When that fad disappeared, they lowered their hemlines and kept pace with the next fad. (It's interesting and significant that the latest fad is often the opposite extreme of the one just before it; the maxi follows the mini.)

People maintaining a balanced outlook in Catholic education must beware of fads too. It's just as silly to throw out all established structure and move with the latest fad as it is to throw out all those clothes for the miniskirt. Teachers long ago discovered that if they hold onto some basic educational procedures, the procedures often come back in style again.

One other aspect of fads should make practical parents and educators cautious. Fads are, of course, often created by sales people. This is the Madison Avenue side of education. If an equipment salesman talks a principal into some "hardware" before the staff really knows what to do with it, the school may be stuck when the fad passes. A high percentage of change on the fashion scene is created by people simply to sell more clothes. And somewhat the same motivation prompts a lot of educational faddishness too.

Nostalgia and fads, therefore, create their own kind of dilemma. In summarizing some alternative educational directions for Catholics in the light of the current school crisis, there's a problem. Is it possible to discover some new approaches that are as traditional as they should be (to be sound), and yet are creative and innovative at the same time? Is it possible to be educationally sound while experimentally introducing new insights into an educational program?

The key here lies in the field of scientific research. We do have the tools now to evaluate new programs. If you are trying a new educational approach, the educator only has to set up control groups: one uses the new approach, and the other matched group doesn't. By closely following the progress of each group and evaluating this progress scientifically (with tests, interviews, etc.), it is possible to judge whether the new educational approach is really an improvement. Not all educational new ideas pass this performance test. Of course, this scientific method is not the *sole* criteria for evaluation.

However, our third factor must be experimentation and evaluation.

The key to experimentation lies in having a balanced view. One can either be experiment-happy, or one can be afraid of risking the results of experimentation. Perhaps the Church has tended to be timid about experimentation; this fear may come with a natural desire to protect and preserve her sacred traditions.

However, Catholic education cannot survive without experimentation and evaluation. If you eliminate these two concepts, you pose a greater threat to vigorous growth in Catholic education than if you quadrupled the costs. High costs constitute a major problem for Catholic education. However, it won't even be worthwhile paying the bills if Catholic education is not free to grow and develop creatively. This imaginative growth depends upon valid experimental programs.

What do we mean specifically by the word experimentation? What would be some examples of this procedure in operation?

Actually, educational experiments are very similar to the research and development occurring in business, medicine, and other areas. The medical world spends much of its time on the primary task of taking care of people who are ill and easing their pain. At the same time, however, many scientific teams are dedicated to improving present medical programs by working in laboratories developing and testing new techniques. This experimentation is the very foundation of progress in medicine. It is vital to all programs aimed at easing pain and saving lives. Millions of people share in the benefits of such research without even thinking about it or being aware that it is going on. The discovery of the polio vaccine is just one dramatic example of this experimental research.

The same thing is true of experimentation in education. You cannot grow creatively unless you continually conduct research experiments. If such research is important in fields like business and commerce, how much more important it should be in a business with learning as its product. If experimentation can give us polio cures and kitchen conveniences, why shouldn't it also have an impact on our whole system of education? As we noted earlier, obsolescence in the classroom is as serious as using unsafe, out-of-date cars. This does not necessarily mean that all traditional practices will become obsolete. It does mean, however, that education will grow and improve only if some experimentation is permitted to feed and foster that growth and excellence.

However, we must beware of the fads.

Therefore, there is another component that must accompany and balance experimental procedures. That concept is evaluation.

Although the average person may not know a great deal about control groups and testing programs, we are all evaluating throughout most of our lives. (Any woman shopper who compares prices and products in a supermarket is engaged in the evaluation process.)

Experimentation programs running wild can be just as harmful as no experimentation. But experiments that are tested and evaluated constantly will feed back new educational concepts into the learning system. This experimental procedure makes educational growth possible.

How does such evaluation work?

Suppose some university professor comes up with an idea that he thinks will revolutionize the teaching of mathematics in elementary schools. He thinks out some of the aspects of his new teaching method and probably writes a few articles about his theory in some professional magazines. Maybe he will write a book on the theory and other educators can comment on his approach, or even critically evaluate it.

Somewhere during this process, the ideas should be tested with some elementary school children and their teachers. So the professor probably gets permission from some public and private schools to have their students use his new curriculum materials for a period of time. He then sets up a standard experimental procedure used to validate his findings.

He will set up matched groups of students—classes that have similar IQ levels, economic backgrounds, etc. This artificial grouping is created solely for research purposes and ceases to exist when the evaluation is concluded. The experimental groups will probably be given a test so their performance can be recorded scientifically just before they start using the experimental teaching materials.

Some of the classes will study math the traditional way and some of the matched groups will use the new curriculum materials. The experiment can involve a few classes in one school, or it may involve hundreds of classrooms in various parts of the country.

After a certain period of time—it could be a few months or several years—tests are administered to the classes participating in the experiment. When these tests are compared with the test scores at the beginning of the experiment, our college professor can scientifically document just how effective his new math method was.

This approach can be as convincing and objective as the work of a laboratory technician in a hospital whose experiments might have helped in finding a cure for cancer. Both experiments are studied closely so the findings can be shared with others and thus contribute to future growth in the field of medicine or education.

If our college professor has dramatic results, his next step is to get increased attention in the educational books and magazines. Perhaps a publishing company will want to print his new approach in a textbook, or a commercial company may translate his concept to film or other audiovisual materials.

These companies will then promote this new math method. If school systems buy the new materials and teachers like them, a new curriculum approach will have been born. The modern math your children study was developed in just this way.

Naturally, the scientific analysis must be ongoing. Even if a new concept is valid and valuable now, it may become out-dated by new and more valuable approaches developed in other experiments.

It may seem to parents that there would be a constant state of flux in classrooms as a result of experimentation and evaluation. Generally, however, this is not the case. The basic educational procedure remains relatively stable for most children, with very few dramatic new changes. It is rarely a revolution; rather it's a gradual evolution—with changes being integrated into the classroom slowly.

Those re-designing Catholic education are making hazardous guesses unless their theories and new approaches are constantly buttressed by the scientific analysis of experimentation and evaluation. It is the worst kind of leadership to damage students and schools in the process of seeking "gimmicks" that are not scientifically sound.

ADMINISTRATIVE CHANGES

In beginning our analysis of specific changes to be made in Catholic education in America, we should start at the top, for the question of leadership is a crucial one.

It is quite obvious to most people today that we have a leadership crisis. It's very difficult to define just what it is that constitutes the magic a good leader has, but it's obvious that the people with it are scarce.

People have taken to calling such leadership attraction "charisma." Since it is difficult to define, it's easier just to point to some people who have had it. Winston Churchill is one, John Kennedy and Pope John XXIII are further examples. Among women you could probably point to individuals like Madame Curie or Pearl Buck.

How could charisma solve our school problems? Of course, charisma alone wouldn't solve them, but it could provide us with the people who could serve as "rallying points." Others would gather round these leaders and follow them forward in seeking new approaches to Catholic education.

Recently, someone suggested that what we need is a vigorous voice that says something like "Let's get this country moving again." It moved Americans out of their lethargy in 1960; in many areas Americans need to be snapped out of a mood of defeatism and despair. And it is not enough to say to Catholics: "We need our schools; we must save our schools." Effective leadership demands specific plans for action in saving schools. The Catholic community wants a plan. They want their leaders to state specifically: "This is what we will do to solve the problem."

With reference to the Catholic school leadership vacuum, in some dioceses the scene approaches the chaotic. Schools often close willy-nilly, with no organized pattern that takes into account diocesan-wide or regional needs. (In some instances, the pastor alone makes the decision to close a school. This represents the worst kind of injustice to the people who have built and maintained the school, as well as the faculty and students who have made it a functioning reality.)

Any psychologist will verify that when a crisis exists, there is often a strong need for leadership guidelines. Decisions reached alone and under pressure, are often the wrong decisions.

The leadership vacuum is slowly being filled. Leadership roles are, once again, following previous public-school patterns. The crisis can be eased somewhat if a diocese institutes an effective Board of Education.

The Catholic School Board

Guidelines for the development of a Board of Education can be found in a practical booklet entitled *Voice of the Community—The Board Movement in Catholic Education.*[22] And a practical handbook for board members also has been published.[23] Both references are vital for leaders involved in forming and administering diocesan school boards.

The concept of a school board for Catholic schools goes back historically to the nineteenth century. The Third Plenary Council of Baltimore in 1884, called for the appointment of an educational committee in each diocese. However, due to the administrative power of the local bishops, diocesan educational committees never got off the ground. Recently, however, spurred by current administrative deficiencies, almost half of the dioceses in the United States have formed boards.

Usually, to get administrative re-organization started, the local bishop will appoint members to a diocesan Board of Education. The eventual goal would be to have the board consist of an elected membership. The board should truly represent the community it serves, so clergy and laity should be members. Generally a three-year term is suggested on a staggered basis so one-third of the members are elected each year.

Quite naturally, the increased involvement of lay people in the educational administration of parishes and dioceses will bring problems. Apathy for one thing; inexperience for another. However, clergy who use this as an excuse for not involving the laity are being unfair to the community they are called upon to serve. Historically, the Church has not given lay people much practice in the fine art of leadership. Why, then, blame the laity when they simply reflect this lack of experience?

The Church must provide in-service education (workshops, etc.) to train lay leaders. This could be done on closed-circuit television where a diocese has access to such a communications system. Eventually, the people will have the background required to do the job effectively. But this will require patience on the part of both clergy and laity. The Church has the right to expect this patience from both.

There is apt to be some confusion concerning the function of a diocesan board of education. The board does not exist to *administer* the schools or other educational programs; instead, it formulates the official educational policies of the diocese. The board retains an administrator (a Secretary of Education) to achieve, by rules, what the board legislates as policy.

Thus, in setting forth its policies, the board provides educational guidelines for the diocese. It is up to the Education Secretary, Superintendent of Schools, the CCD Director, etc., to carry out these policies. The board will severely curtail its leadership capability if it lowers itself to the role of administrative rule-making.

For example, the Board of Education would legitimately concern itself with policies such as: what schools should be established or discontinued; what religious orders should be invited to staff specific schools or catechetical centers; the approval of building sites for educational centers; the community relations of all educational operations in the diocese; and other similar policy areas. The board will not become involved in the detailed administration of operating any specific school.

In order to coordinate all educational departments of the diocese, it is strongly urged that the diocesan board of education be a true board of education and not merely a school board. Within the scope of its responsibility should fall all formal educational activities of the Church within the diocese. "While this word 'formal' is subject to many interpretations, it is used here to exclude such educational and formational activities as cursillo, retreats, etc. Definitely included under the authority of the board should be all catechetical instructions, adult education and the educational aspects of the Newman Apostolate. *This concept of a diocesan board of education is essential to the unification of the educational effort within a diocese."* [24] (Emphasis added)

The board should have standing committees as consultants, for example, in the areas of financial affairs, inner-city programs, communications, and public relations. These consultants would not be board members, but would function in a service capacity for the board.

The diocesan Director (or Secretary) of Education would be responsible for administering all educational programs in the diocese, and would execute the board's policies. Both the board and the Director of Education should be advisory to the bishop, who is the final authority in the diocese. It is obvious, however, that the effective sharing of this authority is the key to all Catholic educational growth.

Another practical administrative approach to providing unity in the diocese could be the concept of a cabinet, as it is employed by America's President. To unify all educational departments within the diocese, it might be helpful to have regular cabinet meetings—perhaps monthly. These could be presided over by the Director of Education or the bishop. It would give the Superintendent of Schools, the Assistant Superintendents, the CCD Director and his assistants, the seminaries, the campus ministry—all education departments—an opportunity to compare problems and plan solutions jointly.

This group would not function as a Board of Education, but instead, would constitue a working team of administrators regularly attacking specific joint problems with unity and coordination. This would also help insure that an educational consensus is formed, rather than that everything depend solely upon the judgment of the Director of Education.

I suppose, like the British and Canadian systems of government, one could *unite* the administrative and policy-making roles. In this case, your Cabinet would *be* your Board of Education. Our American government model usually separates the two.

The board movement, like so many aspects of Catholic education, involves a delicate balance between increasing centralization of authority and "grass roots" participation. It is obvious that the advantages of an education board would apply at the parish and regional levels also. Thus, there will be parish education boards and, eventually, area boards of education. A system-wide solution to educational problems is possible only when these problems are studied and solved on a *regional* basis. Thus, in the long run, the grass-roots education boards will be area or regional boards—not individual parish groups. Such area boards encourage the solution of problems in the light of the needs of a region, without having each parish operating independently.

Consolidation

In a *Saturday Review* education feature (July, 1972), Louis Gary and K.C. Cole state candidly:

> ... contributions, or the government are not going to help the
> Catholic schools until Church leaders stop concentrating their
> efforts on keeping schools open that will close in a few years
> anyway. Instead of continuing to preserve buildings, *Church leaders*
> *should begin to preserve the option of Catholic education itself.*
> (Emphasis added)
> This means they must close inefficient schools and consolidate the
> system.

Centralization—or consolidation—is the real challenge in creating a system-wide solution to educational problems in the Church. In many aspects of our lives we have seen a move toward centralized authority. Although it is resented by some, it almost seems as if it is the price we must pay for progress.

A regional approach involves a geographical area, including a number of cities and towns—not an area as wide as the New England region.

The regional approach concerning Catholic education refers to a plan linking various parishes in an area; the diocese itself would consist of a number of such regions.

Most city planners are beginning to realize that major urban problems require a regional metropolitan planning approach. Our inner cities were once separated from the suburbs and all the local cities and towns worked out their own problems individually. They wanted it this way; it was more American keeping local control.

However, it's easy to see what's beginning to happen in terms of growth and population density. As suburbs explode we will soon have one large area of central population sprawling from the inner city areas and rolling over suburb after suburb. As this happens, you really have one huge metropolitan area consisting of many cities and towns all thrown together by problems they share: transportation, sewage, pollution, taxes, crime and violence.

For each small segment of this metropolitan area to try to solve these problems alone is a silly duplication of effort. However, if there were a metropolitan planning commission, and these cities and towns were represented, with the authority to make policy decisions and act on them, the whole area could combine its resources and attack major problems together. It is difficult to surrender some of this local autonomy, but it is also hard to stand by and watch serious problems destroy people and the quality of life.

A similar quandary faces educators in general. Many people are opposed to greatly increasing state and federal involvement in education. And, to a degree, some local control is surrendered when such larger-scale aid is accepted. However, it has become obvious that educational problems and costs are so extensive and so serious that cities and towns cannot solve them without resorting to broader cooperative effort.

Also, if our country is serious about giving equal opportunity to all, we must be dissatisfied with the great disparity between the unequal educational choices Americans have. If a child lives in a town where $435 per pupil is spent on education, he doesn't have the same educational advantages as a child living in a town spending $835 per pupil on education, assuming equal efficiency, similar cost-of-living, etc. Many people feel state and federal educational aid must equalize this opportunity. Local authorities can't do it alone. And recent court decisions have indicated that such inequalities are unconstitutional, depriving students of equal educational opportunities.

The application of consolidation principles to educational development can best be explained by asking the question: "What ever happened to the little red schoolhouse?"

The small rural school house was not just a picturesque part of our early educational history in America; it performed a valid and valuable service. As our American public-school system grew and developed, however, it became obvious that if you organized across county lines and developed larger regional school districts, taxpayers could build better schools for their children. And children could travel in a bus to these larger, more efficient schools. (Did you ever see a science lab in a little red schoolhouse?)

This whole movement reflected a consolidation of many small schools into larger school districts, managed by broader regional administrative units.

This process is now facing the Church if its school system is to have any meaning in the years ahead. Some very small schools can no longer function validly, just as the little red schoolhouse can't. Several parishes must now consolidate their schools and work jointly on educational programs, thus eliminating much wasteful duplication.

With diocesan-wide planning, a system can be set up whereby the diocese is divided into regional areas. Then within each region, elementary schools act as feeder-schools for the regional high school.

A specific example of this type of consolidation can be seen in an exhaustive study of the Catholic school system of the Archdiocese of Boston.[25] The Boston study was conducted by the New England Catholic Education Center (NECEC), and was commissioned by the late Cardinal Cushing. It provides a scientific basis for the necessary reorganization of the schools in the largest educational system, public or private, in the whole New England area.

In conducting the research study, NECEC utilized many resources: university scholars, a major public-opinion poll organization, legal firms, and computerized information retrieval systems. When the completed study was turned over to Church authorities, NECEC had provided guidelines, or a blueprint for the consolidation of Catholic schools in the Archdiocese of Boston.

With a minimum dislocation of pupils, the study recommended a unified school system run by a central Board of Education and organized into eight or nine regional districts, each with its own high school. The consolidated elementary schools in each region would act as "feeder schools" for the regional high schools.

In Chicago the School Study Commission urged decentralization, and a rearrangement of the school-parish relationship, including independent administration and fiscal responsibility.

What effect does consolidation have upon enrollment figures? This will vary. In Des Moines when the diocese consolidated around district lines, the officials felt there were very few students who could not be taken care of by bussing to near-by schools. Quite frankly, this will not always be the case.

This leads to a very practical question: How can Catholic school officials and public school administrators plan together for this transfer of pupils? In fairness to students and their parents, education officials should do everything possible to minimize the trauma of such a transition. Administratively this might even require a new educational specialist. In the light of the 1971 Supreme Court decision, the most critical challenge facing Catholic education will be this need to restructure itself. Yet, while this vast re-organization is taking place, many on-going educational needs must be met. The diocesan Superintendent of Schools must continue to work out teacher-staffing problems, curriculum renewal and countless other professional tasks. The Director of Education, meanwhile, must be moving forward with the plans to coordinate Catholic schools, CCD, adult education, and other educational programs under a cooperative Catholic education umbrella. Then who can assume responsibility for working closely with public school officials in arrangements for new Catholic school districts, closings, leasing of Catholic schools, etc.?

I would recommend that a specialist handle consolidation exclusively. Such a full-time consultant could be called a Liaison Coordinator. The role of this administrator would be to coordinate all the consolidation machinery. Directly representing the local bishop, and working closely with the Catholic Superintendent of Schools and the diocesan Director of Education, this Coordinator also would work with public-school officials. Thus, by directly representing the bishop in this one area, the consultant removes this burden from both the Director of Education and the Superintendent of Schools.

This would be a full-time position for about four or five years as plans are reformulated for various Catholic schools. In some geographical areas, it will mean closing schools; in some locales, it might mean leasing to public school officials; in some communities, it could mean developing shared-time programs between Catholic schools and public schools.

To insure "grass-roots" participation in this process, the Liaison Coordinator would establish Advisory Councils, drawn up around geographical regions. These Councils could consist of regional leaders — pastors, public and Catholic school principals, parental representatives, etc. Such regional cooperation would help develop plans that would meet the varying educational needs of different locales.

It is essential that the role of the Liaison Coordinator be filled by an educational professional. It might be practical to hire a Catholic who has been a public-school administrator (maybe a Superintendent of Schools); such a person already has a working knowledge of public school policies and personnel. The position would no longer exist after the consolidation phase had been completed. At that time, the Church would have a school system integrated in various ways with public-school systems, thus relieving the current financial crisis.

In many states the size of the consolidation task will also demand that the State Department of Education appoint a special administrator to act as a state consultant on consolidation problems. The Commonwealth of Massachusetts has already appointed such a consultant. One aftermath of the latest Supreme Court decision will most likely be many similar appointments.

Consolidation means that some of the local control will be surrendered, but representation can be provided if local committees (parish education committees, for example) assist the diocesan school authorities with decisions affecting their own local areas. A central vantage point insures however, that good plans are not defeated by lack of imagination, or "vested interests" on the local level.

The concept of consolidation does carry a price tag, because some local control is lost. But parishes might discover that, in surrendering some of their local jurisdiction over schools, they are gaining more than they lose: all educational problems are no longer the burden of one parish alone. These challenges can be shared by many shoulders and the money needed to solve the problems can come from a broader base too.

Forming an Educational System

Ahead of us lies the whole thrust of the movement to centralize the administration of the Catholic educational program into a system. As the Boston study mentioned above documents, the financial structure of school support simply must be broadened. Just as small towns are looking to the state and federal government for help, individual parishes need regional or diocesan-wide financial support. This has been done to some degree in the past, with wealthier suburban parishes helping inner-city churches. However, today the whole financial structure must be more explicitly diocesan-wide.

With specific reference to education, if Catholic education is to grow in the future, it will be forced to adapt a fiscally unified accounting and budgetary system. Such a fiscal system must be compatible with public school accounting procedures. This will permit full accountability and easy access to financial data, if public funds are ever to be used by Catholic schools.

The current situation is summarized by one writer this way: ". . . we do not claim that the cost figures given by any Catholic school authority today represent the precise cost of Catholic education. Such figures will be accurate only when a uniform system of cost accounting is required of all schools and the figures are subject to independent audit to be sure that the system is being consistently followed by all concerned. This does not imply dishonesty. Whatever cost figures are obtainable are honestly reported. Accurate figures are simply not obtainable because of the lack of modern cost accounting."[26]

There is a need to offset this kind of fiscal naivete which worked well in the past, but won't be functional any longer. One approach is to establish a diocesan school fund which might possibly be fiscally independent of the Church.

The New York Archdiocese, under the direction of Cardinal Cooke, has taken some practical steps in this direction. They have been analyzed in print by Monsignor George A. Kelly.[27]

Until recently, the effectiveness of the Superintendent of Schools and the CCD Director was seriously limited by lack of funds. The power and status of each office was limited by an inadequate budget.

To meet the fiscal demands, each office received a significantly increased budget, along with a responsible role in the fund raising. "While fund raising will not be a direct function in the Office of Educational Finance in the foreseeable future, the Office of Educational Finance will, of necessity, work as a member of the fund-raising group for education now being formed. . . . The Office of Educational Finance will have the responsibility of providing . . . the financial needs of the Department of Education. Likewise . . . it will be involved in a similar way in other fund-raising endeavors . . . it will be responsible for the budgeting, management, and disbursement of educational funds received from all sources. This is essential in order to insure that the Department of Education will be in a position to properly manage the funding of its educational programs."[28]

New York provides a model for other diocesan educational administrators in applying modern management principles to the Church's educational programs. This might not have happened if a crisis hadn't forced it; the important thing is that it is happening.

Another diocese providing administrative leadership is Dubuque, Iowa. The document explaining the reorganization of its Catholic educational structures into geographical areas provides specific organizational details.[29] This reorganization, too, offers a model for administrators faced with the same administrative and consolidation needs.

Educational Cooperation

There is another administrative challenge facing Catholic educators. This is the challenge of *cooperation*.

When Catholic schools began, one of the reasons for their establishment was the blatant anti-Catholic nature of America's public school system. If we are to be honest, we must admit that the relationship between public schools and Catholic school personnel has not always been cordial. Until recent years, there hasn't been much cooperative effort between them.

For many reasons, this has changed, and ought to continue to change. Today's public schools are obviously secular. Catholic educational personnel have a personal commitment to Christ and to a Christian witness. At the same time, Catholic schools can work on joint educational programs with public-school authorities. This will benefit both administrations, and it will especially serve the students of both systems.

We have discussed earlier the administrative leadership required in the consolidation process. Here we should examine some specific procedures as they apply to the increasing educational cooperation necessary in Catholic education.

Let's imagine three adjoining suburban towns that constitute a region and examine how cooperative consolidation can be organized and executed. Our imaginative region includes:

3 public high schools
4 public junior high schools
12 public elementary schools
2 Catholic parish high schools
and 6 Catholic parish elementary schools.

In working out a Catholic school consolidation pattern for this regional area, the Catholic officials simply *must* consult with local public officials, both for information concerning local needs, and also to facilitate good public relations and efficient planning for all concerned.

A diocesan Liaison Coordinator (mentioned above) could supervise this restructuring, but there probably would be a regional chairman who would work more closely with local leadership. This chairman probably should be a Catholic school representative so a certain amount of educational professionalism would provide the dynamic leadership the local community requires.

The grass roots committee working with the chairman and the diocesan Liaison Coordinator might have the following representation:

a public high school principal
a junior high school principal
a representative from the public Superintendent of School's office from each of the three towns
the principal of each Catholic school involved
the pastor of each parish school involved
a representative from an area clergy association
a representative from the School Committees of each of the three towns
PTA representation
a lawyer
and a financial consultant

Such a local working committee gives wide community representation. It would be too large, probably, to constitute an active working committee, but it does provide for listening to the voice of the people. The group might elect an Executive Committee that could meet more frequently for the concentrated work and then report back to the entire group regularly.

When such a committee is called together the diocesan Liaison Coordinator and the regional chairman should have prepared a skeletal reorganization pattern, based on larger regional and even diocesan-wide needs. This also provides a specific suggested consolidation that the community leaders can react to.

Obviously if such a reorganizational pattern is stiffly formalized and inflexible, it is a farce to pretend that you plan to listen to community voices. It will be impossible to please all of the people all of the time with the new educational structure. However, there must be a real flexibility so your final regional re-organization will incorporate local suggestions and answer local and regional needs.

How does one arrive at the first meeting with a skeletal plan?

One way is to have a professional organization draw up a diocesan-wide re-organization pattern. (This was done in the Archdiocese of Boston, for example, by the Stanwick Corporation and incorporated into the NECEC study submitted to Cardinal Cushing.) This management analysis gives you a framework from which to operate. It might be wise to schedule a meeting with your regional Catholic representatives first. This provides an opportunity to discuss the ramifications of the proposed framework on local Catholic schools, parishes, etc.

Initially, your entire committee should probably be notified of the meeting shortly in advance of the date. This helps to insure accuracy and cut down on the damage and panic a rash of rumors can cause. The committee representatives thus have a specific reorganization plan before wild stories get circulated among the area families.

The committee can then react to the plan with suggestions in the light of special community problems, especially with a view to public-school needs (school building plans, individual public-school enrollments), as well as financial conditions in local Catholic parishes, diocesan educational and financial commitments, etc.

The groups should have timetables that are both efficient and realistic. Grass roots democracy is not noted for its speed. Several school committees are involved, and new school bonding issues must be debated by the citizens whose taxes are affected by consolidation procedures. But the groups should begin with a timetable in mind and try to stand by the deadlines suggested.

Under the regional chairman's direction, the Executive Committee might draft a regional proposal taking into consideration the basic skeletal outline suggested by diocesan officials, and the suggestions of the regional committee members. This proposal could be referred back to the diocesan Liaison Coordinator for action.

If grass roots participation is to have any meaning, Church leaders must listen to local voices, remembering that "the people" *are* "the Church." Whenever possible, the new structures should reflect special area needs. And if possible, Catholic educational leaders should work out their programs in conjunction with local public-school leaders. This educational openness offers enrichment for everybody involved.

Therefore, our imaginary three-suburban-town area might emerge with the following changes after the local consolidation consultation process:

One Catholic parish high school will close (the building will be converted by the parish into an educational community center);

of the six local Catholic elementary schools, only three will remain open (one will be torn down, one will be leased to town officials, and one will be purchased outright by the town).

A bussing program can be instituted so that Catholic school pupils from the schools that are closing can be transported to the nearest Catholic schools remaining open. Catholic officials assume a few parents will not want their child bussed and will enroll them, instead, in their neighborhood public school. However, a poll conducted in the process of the committee's work indicated that most parents would not withdraw their children. The consolidation plan would continue to provide Catholic-school education for about 45 percent of all students currently in the local Catholic schools. This is true because in several parish schools that closed, there were many empty classrooms before the consolidation phase began.

The remaining 55 percent of the Catholic elementary school population would be absorbed into the public school program. This increase would be accomplished by the one leased school, the one purchased school, and existing public-school expansion plans. Perhaps some of the Catholic school teachers would also be absorbed into these consolidated schools.

The Catholic elementary schools remaining open would draw their financial support from all parishes served by these regional elementary schools and from diocesan educational funds. All regional parish officials would also plan an expanded CCD program and adult education programs to supplement the work continuing at the Catholic schools in the area.

This fictitious plan simply serves as a specific guideline for a consolidation. This type of consolidation should be occurring along regional lines all over America. The 1971 Supreme Court decision against paying teacher salaries in Catholic schools means that such specific cooperative consolidation plans should become reality as soon as possible.

Probably people close to many parish administrators are shaking their heads and saying sadly: "It's unrealistic to think of pastors and parishioners supporting educational programs outside their own parish." Often, however, quite unwilling change is forced upon pastors by circumstances beyond their control. Limited financial resources will continue to make Catholics much more regionally oriented than they were "in the good old days." With their backs to the wall, financially, administrators will be surprised to see how much better it is to cooperate with one another on a regional basis.

Nonpublic and public schools have recently found themselves cooperating on educational programs for the first time because there were federal funds involved and the government required such cooperative planning in order to obtain the money. Such cooperation need not be limited to programs requiring it fiscally. Probably the future of Catholic education in America will include many integrated educational programs.

One practical example would be the increased practice of public-school authorities leasing Catholic school buildings. This move requires joint administrative decisions, and people who haven't worked closely together before, find they are solving problems jointly now.

DUAL ENROLLMENT

The most dramatic example of cooperative effort is an educational innovation that has been growing slowly, but hasn't received the kind of attention it deserves. It is a concept that could solve many of the current Catholic educational problems, but it requires a lot of administrative finesse. It's known as shared time, or dual enrollment. In addition to financial advantages, it has educational and social benefits as well. This could be part of the current thrust to go *beyond* the classroom. This isn't fragmentation; it's enrichment.

This concept will undoubtedly be subject to legal scrutiny to avoid constitutional pitfalls. All shared-time administrators should be familiar with the text of the 1971 Supreme Court *Lemon* and *DiCenso* cases to avoid such pitfalls.

Dual enrollment simply means that nonpublic schools send their pupils to public schools for instruction in one or more subjects during the regular school day. The procedure might also be called split time, reserved time, shared time enrollment, educational cooperation, part-time enrollment, or dual registration.

The concept can be traced back to Thomas Jefferson. He suggested that various denominations build divinity schools near the University of Virginia. Students could then attend the University for secular subjects and take theological studies at their own schools.

A student may spend part of his school day in his parish school, studying religion, history, ethics, and other subjects. Then he would walk (or be bussed) to a nearby public school where he could make use of a magnificent science lab, a language lab, and study under public school math teachers.

Say, for instance, that there is an eighth-grade student who has a interest in a medical career, or the profession of engineering. Some Catholic secondary schools simply cannot supply the scientific laboratories this student deserves. He can now get the benefit from the educational opportunities available at a nearby public school (as he should, since *his* parents' taxes too have built the public school).

However, a doctor and an engineer must have their view of man matured along with their study of the machine. A philosophy of man—his origin, nature, and destiny—all can be supplied by the Church through a dynamic educational program. A religious context for the learning process has always been the goal of Catholic education. Perhaps, if some Catholic schools are freed from the responsibility of teaching mathematics and science, they can spread their limited resources out to reach more people. Instead of providing the whole educational program for a very limited number of individuals, parish funds can provide the religious and ethical basis of learning for most people. And upon this foundation constructed by the religious school, the public school can build a solid secular structure.

Other educational innovations could be a part of the shared-time approach. Evening classes could be added to the school day and classes could be spread out (as college classes are), some as early as 8:00 a.m. and some going into the late afternoon or evening hours.

Shared time could give Catholic students the best of both worlds; but it's obvious that this plan has potential problems too. Some of these problems have been overcome by several school systems.

The concepts of experimentation and evaluation we discussed earlier have been applied to this educational innovation. One of the most complete research studies constructed around shared time has been done in Chicago.[30] In this case, a Catholic high school was designed and built especially to provide participants in a shared-time program.

In 1964 and 1965 the Chicago Board of Education authorized a shared-time experiment that included the John F. Kennedy Public School and St. Paul's (Catholic) High School. The experiment covered a four-year period, so the school board could analyze the growth of students entering the shared-time program as freshmen (in 1965) until their graduation in 1969.

The evaluation was designed to measure objectively the effect of the program on the students, and to assess the reactions of the parents, students, and teachers who participated in the program.

This shared-time experiment is probably the largest such high-school program in the nation, and, therefore, received a great deal of attention. In June, 1969, approximately 132 students graduated, having attended a Chicago public high-school and a nonpublic high school concurrently.

These students took English, social studies, and religion at St. Paul's, and all other subjects, including physical education, art and music at Kennedy. The students spent approximately the same amount of time at each school. When the shared-time graduates were compared with those who had attended Kennedy full-time the following factors emerged, significantly, in the shared-time students.

They possessed, on the average, greater general ability; they took more college-prep courses, received higher grades, were absent less, and received about the same scores on college admissions tests. They also participated in fewer extra-curricular activities at the public high school and were elected to fewer offices there. (This indicates that one of the difficulties of a shared-time program is that it might create a problem of divided loyalty in high-school students who often need such school loyalty during adolescence.) Being loyal to two schools can present a special challenge to young people. Probably, not all would be capable of the challenge. On the other hand, of course, sometimes intense school loyalty has less desirable aspects, and this competitive push would be decreased if a student broadened his horizons to include two schools.

In general the administrators, parents and students who participated in the Chicago shared-time program reacted favorably to it. Programming problems and longer days were the two items about which most of the parents and students were concerned, but almost all of them indicated that they would recommend the shared-time program to friends or relatives who are about to begin high school.

There was no evidence in the study that the shared-time programs in which the Chicago public high school participated had, in any observable or measurable way, a harmful or detrimental effect on students or on the public-school system of the city of Chicago.

A unique shared-time program has also developed in Swanton, Vermont, and has been called "a very valuable piece of educational pioneering" by the Vermont Council of Churches.

In a letter to this author, a local school official described their approach. "We are developing in Swanton, Vermont, a unique educational program which will combine public and private services and facilities within a single educational complex. The private facility, physically and administratively separate from the public building, will be used primarily for religious instruction by all religious denominations for children of all religious faiths, and therefore, will be ecumenically owned and operated. Three public high schools and one parochial high school are phasing out their separate educational facilities and combining the best features of public and private education within a single public school system in which all children will be enrolled. The private facility, built on privately owned land adjacent to the public building, will be privately maintained, operated, staffed, etc., and will offer religion courses on a voluntary, elec--tive and non-coercive basis to all children five days a week, seven periods a day."[31]

The Vermont administrator adds: "This project is the first of its kind in in the nation and is being promoted as an answer to two problems: education for all children and . . . a religious ecumenical education to be provided for all children within the framework of our public-school system, yet guarantee our cherished separation of church and state. We feel that this plan will be an answer to one of the nation's greatest dilemmas. This project has been featured in national magazines and has been viewed nationally both on CBS and the NBC television network."

The National Education Association has conducted a nationwide survey of shared-time programs.[32] When they asked participating superintendents if they would recommend shared time in the light of their experiences, 63 percent of the superintendents said "yes." (28 percent did not answer, and 9 percent said "no.")

The NEA summed up basic arguments for shared time:

It broadens educational opportunities for Catholic school students.
It provides a good relationship between public and nonpublic schools.
It results in greater support of public schools by Catholics.
It is a way out of the controversy over public aid for nonpublic schools.
It eases the Catholic-school critical financial situation.
It gives Catholic students an opportunity to spend some time in a pluralistic environment.

Arguments against this concept include:

It may have constitutional difficulties.
Administrative problems might prove insurmountable.
It may have a detrimental effect on public schools.
It may have a detrimental effect on private schools.
It does not present a solution to the controversy.

Some Catholic educators have identified potential difficulties from the viewpoint of Catholic schools. One such problem is that there are literally thousands of nuns and brothers trained to teach subjects like science and math. What do you do with these professionals? One solution may lie in a practice already growing among Catholic educators. Many nuns are already contracting to teach secular subjects, for which they are prepared, in public schools, in order to bolster sagging financial resources within their religious community. Such a sister would continue to live in a religious community and would turn over her salary to the community as her own contribution to its work.

Other Catholic observers see shared time as a serious threat to the unity of Catholic educational programs, with their desired emphasis upon

The real goal of a sound curriculum is to train a student's mind and sharpen his ability to learn. Learning, therefore, can continue throughout his life because the student's educational years have given him the necessary tools—a mind that can analyze and think critically. How else can today's young people and adults cope with the decisions and evaluations facing them? Whether it is a matter of *grasping* political arguments, or a matter of *analyzing* news reports, or critically *evaluating* a TV commercial—education should have provided the equipment: a trained mind.

Independent study techniques are exemplified best by new curriculum approaches, such as team-teaching, ungraded classes, flexible modular scheduling (which breaks long class periods into more flexible short periods, or "modes"), and the open classroom concept. All of these curriculum innovations are attempts to break away from the staid situation of a teacher standing in front of a number of students—the approach often referred to as the "talking face."

Most parents are first made aware of a drastic curriculum change when their child comes home for some help with his arithmetic. The parent then runs into something called "the new math."

Such curriculum innovations are not designed simply to frustrate the parental generation. Rather, the goal is to train the younger generation to grasp underlying concepts of math, such as sets and systems. Thus, instead of rote learning, the child is acquiring understanding. This understanding can then be applied to other situations.

A basic challenge facing educators today is the rapid rate at which today's facts turn into tomorrow's fictions—the knowledge simply becomes outdated. No wonder teachers ask: "Why should we insist on students memorizing facts that will no longer be true soon after the students graduate?"

However, a mind trained to think and analyze logically, and human understanding, will almost always be valuable; if times change, a well-trained mind can adapt to new ideas and seek new solutions. It is almost impossible for us to predict the problems to be faced by today's youth as they mature into adulthood. How can we prepare them for unknown contingencies by providing them with fact after fact?

In an English class, for example, as students and teacher study *Long Day's Journey Into Night*, the goal is not to memorize the names of the characters, but to develop critical judgment as a reader, and to evaluate the play in terms of human understanding, current student needs, viewpoints and aspirations. After all, the teacher will not always be available to explain what a play means. When young people leave the classroom, they should have developed this ability.

The teacher's goal, therefore, is to develop a sensitivity to beauty and form so the student has a feel for good literature, good movies, good theater. This trained judgment will be enriching an individual's life long after he has forgotten the symbolic meaning of fog in Eugene O'Neill's play. As a teacher I have often warned students that the goal of their studying with me is to enable them to get along very well without me. The goal of all education is for students to outgrow their teachers—just as parents should also train their children toward a maturity that will make the young adult capable of responsible action without the parent. Educators and parents are engaged in a business designed to put themselves out of business.

Many new educational theories are considered idealistic and unrealistic, and, perhaps, this is just what the educational pioneer should try to be.

For example, teachers who work with disadvantaged children in a ghetto area are probably much more practical than university professors who have no direct practical experience teaching in ghetto schools. However, it is true that many new approaches to learning come from colleges and universities. Academic researchers are free to theorize. As we explained earlier, though, the new approaches the university professors dream of have demonstrated validity only after they have worked in the classroom.

However, we must not be too harsh on the educational theorists. It is also true that many valid educational approaches are not given a fair chance by the classroom teachers. Why?

Let's suppose someone came into your office or plant (an efficiency expert, for example) and told you your working methods were old-fashioned and ineffective. And this "expert" had a new approach that would work well for you.

Suppose you are a housewife and another woman enters your home and insists that your work habits are wasteful and inefficient, or that the way you are raising your children is not sound. In all occupations and professions there are self-styled experts. And it is very human to resent their interference and advice.

But does such resentment always make sense? What if these experts can teach us ways to save time and effort with our tasks?

Returning to the classroom, it's perhaps the normal, natural thing for teachers to resent it when someone says: "Your method is wrong or old-fashioned." Trying to convince educators of the value of new curriculum approaches requires a certain amount of common sense, psychology and patience. Mixed in with these ingredients you have to add a certain amount of pure salesmanship. Educational pioneers must have a good supply of all these traits. It may sound crass, but you do have to sell new ideas to parents and teachers.

What is needed is an open-minded, honest approach whenever anyone hears suggestions that might help improve our schools. Generally the best approach is to evaluate the new educational technique honestly by trying it. A teacher is free to make a responsible judgment if it doesn't work well. Classroom teachers have a right to criticize a new educational approach openly and constructively only after considering seriously and trying it in the classroom.

Educational theorists must realize that there will always be some sort of time-lag between the period when a new educational approach is born and the time it will be accepted widely and used in the classrooms. This time-lag will vary depending upon the quality of the new educational idea, the initial inconvenience it may present to the classroom teacher, and the selling job that's done to put the new idea over.

And we can't forget that just as each housewife decides what is going to go on in her kitchen, classroom teachers have certain rights concerning their classrooms and teaching procedures. There may be curriculum standards established by each school system; there may be directives handed down by the school administrators; there may be pressures from parents—still the classroom teacher is given the responsibility to encourage her students toward a certain level of growth and she is expected to do it. (And, for the most part, she'll do it *her* way!)

These general curriculum innovation concepts present specific challenges to Catholic educators when it comes to making religion classes meaningful. Catholic-school curriculum considerations must include this fourth R—religion. I remember being slightly shocked when I was first told that it's difficult to find nuns who will teach religion in Catholic schools today. My initial reaction was: "If these nuns have a special commitment, and their choice of the religious life would indicate such a commitment, why wouldn't they want to teach religion?"

Gradually I learned that such teachers were apparently afraid of teaching religion to young people precisely because it was so important. They simply felt unequal to the challenge and they didn't want to do an inadequate job on something that was so significant to them. (We might ask *why* these teachers feel inadequate. The answer probably lies in several directions: post-Vatican II changes; insufficient training; and cultural factors, such as the changing attitudes of today's youth. Could it be that religion teachers are born and not made?)

Catholic educators have begun to realize that the same type of professional training they insist upon for the physics teacher is also required for the religion teacher-specialist. During the past few years many teachers have gone back to school to study current approaches to teaching religion. Such a workshop program was held at Boston College in 1971 for example, and the university received many more applications than it could accept. Such graduate programs provide the religious education specialist an opportunity to up-date her theology.

Although Catholic schools must reflect excellence in all curriculum areas, their first priority should continue to be the challenge of showing that significant religious truths bring meaning into man's existence. This requires knowledge of the subject matter, but it also requires adapting this subject to today's needs. (This is why many religion teachers have been using the rock opera "Jesus Crhist Superstar" or the musical "Godspell" in their classes. This may be shocking to "Old-Time Religion" teachers, but it has sparked much religious discussion, nonetheless.)

There is a danger, though, that religion teachers can get carried away in a search for "religious relevance." These teachers do their students no service if they take it upon themselves to "water-down" religious realities. The best gift a religion teacher offers youth is a mind capable of evaluating these religious realities with critical vigor. Many teachers say that young people today do not intellectualize enough. This is the real vocation of the *prophet*: to critically evaluate what you love.

To answer the question "Just how much time do students spend studying religion in school?" we can cite a typical analysis. The school format has been altered somewhat since Joseph Fichter's sociological analysis of a parochial school, but this is what Fichter found in his study. A typical eighth grader's time is apportioned as follows: Religion 10 percent; English 37.3 percent; Arithmetic 15 percent; Social Studies 16 percent; Music 6.7 percent; Science and Health 5.3 percent; Art 4 percent; and Recess and Miscellaneous 5.7 percent.

Another aspect of teaching religion is the controversy spurred by the catechetics pioneer, Brother Gabriel Moran. Moran's challenge is that Christianity is an adult religion and our teaching efforts here should lie in adult education. This thesis is calling forth a renewed emphasis in reaching adults.

Psychologists are teaching us new things about teaching religion to youth also. Some modern research seems to indicate that at very early ages, children are simply not capable of absorbing significant moral evaluations. This will, no doubt, affect our religion programs at the elementary level in the future.

Youth themselves have something to say about the teaching they receive. In a survey of sociological research the following significant conclusions were outlined concerning the religious interests of high school youth. ". . . Typically the adolescent embraces both a traditional belief and a not immodest degree of participation in the ritualistic aspects of religion. His level of knowledge has not been systematically assessed but probably is low. In terms of the experiential dimension, his concern and interest in religion, while not clearly measured, appear to be quite high. The developmuent of concern into deep, orthodox faith is not, however, apparently typical. The American adolescent seems reluctant to deny the idea of a supernatural, but, at the same time, is unwilling or unable to yield himself with firm conviction to the hands of the Divine. Perhaps the best label we can apply to the teenager's religious orientation is 'hedging.' He appears to embrace neither nihilism nor firm commitment. Of course, it should be clear that the picture we have drawn from the meager data available is for the 'average' or 'typical' teenager."[33]

Concerning students' reaction to teaching in general, Dr. Gordon Sabine has conducted a special survey on how students rate their teachers. Interestingly enough, this "Youthpoll" indicated that what students want more than anything else in their high school teachers is a person who *cares*. This applies to all teachers, but it certainly has special bearing in a religion classroom.

A major curriculum question for Catholic educators has reference to what is called "the permeation theory." This often evokes different reactions from different educators.

Catholic educators in the past have said that religion should permeate *all* aspects of the curriculum. Thus, Catholic textbooks appeared with references to Catholic doctrine interspersed with arithmetic problems and geography maps. A great deal of this permeation was pure "Madison Avenue." A publisher might help sales to Catholic schools if the book was filled with religious references. Now that the market is changing, publishers are rushing to remove these references.

The permeation principle still divides Catholic educators. Some feel the schools should never concede there is a basic separation between the sacred and the secular—that the only justification for a Catholic school is the fact that all subjects are taught in a Catholic context.

This viewpoint sees the Catholic school as a witness, an example of a different way, one that reflects wholehearted commitment to Christian example. Such educational leaders argue that if this concept of Christian witness is removed from a Catholic school, there is no dynamic reason for its existence.

Others argue that there is no such thing as Catholic algebra, and that Catholics should let public-school authorities teach math and Catholics should concentrate on the subjects dealing most directly with values and religious truths—like English, history and religion.

We can conclude our list of curriculum reflections with reference to some practical curriculum changes Catholic-school superintendents expect to see in Catholic schools in the next few years.[34] These are some of the predictions made in a survey conducted by the superintendents within the National Catholic Educational Association in 1970:

> 95 percent of Catholic secondary schools in the country will be employing forms of modular scheduling.
> 70 percent of the Catholic secondary and elementary schools will be using a form of personal evaluation of student progress rather than a number or letter grade on reports to parents.
> The school day in 50 percent of the Catholic schools will include courses at night for both youth and adults.

50 percent of the dioceses will be in the educational contracting business — either signing contracts with firms to teach some of their subjects, or contracting with the public-school district to teach subjects for them.

The number of adults taking part in adult-education courses sponsored by Catholic schools will triple.

A dramatic instance of curriculum innovation could be cited, as an example of the type of adaptation Catholic schools should consider.

Underway in the diocese of Brooklyn, on an experimental basis, is a cooperative demonstration project in computer-managed individualized instruction. Called PLAN, the program was developed by Westinghouse Learning Corporation as Program for Learning in Accordance with Needs.

Modern technology made this possible. A computer functions as an informational system, recording each student's learning and academic history, along with his program of studies, test scores, etc. The student does not interface directly with the computer; however, the computer monitors the day-by-day progress of every student.

PLAN applies the systems approach to education. Individualized instruction from PLAN's point of view is defined as the assignment of appropriate learning tasks to students according to their needs and abilities, and the assignment of appropriate ways for students to accomplish these learning tasks. So the individualization in this system applies to the assignments and the methods of achieving these assignments, rather than to learning in isolation. Thus, the *procedure* is a technological one. Students may learn through independent study, small group discussions, large group activities, or teacher-led activities, whichever is most appropriate.

The first requirement for a system of individualized instruction is to separate the overall educational program into sets of behavioral objectives that can be assigned as learning tasks to individual students. A second requirement of the system is the development of Teaching-Learning Units (TLU's) that prescribe various learning activities by which the student may accomplish the assigned objectives. The Teaching-Learning Unit is a sheet of paper which sets forth an assignment of about two weeks' work for the student and makes suggestions and references to the learning experiences and currently available instructional materials by which he can accomplish these particular assigned objectives. The third requirement of the system of individualized instruction is a program for the assessment of the performance of students relative to the educational objectives.

The diocese of Brooklyn has made adaptations in the basic PLAN concept for use in selected elementary schools. Rev. Michael Dempsey, Brooklyn's Secretary of Education feels this is the type of educational innovation Catholic schools cannot afford *not* to undertake. With fewer teachers required, and with the use of paraprofessionals, the Catholic school can actually cut back on its high personnel costs while improving the school program for students. It will actually cost less to operate such Catholic schools after just a few years of PLAN participation. If the Brooklyn trial is successful, a new type of curriculum could emerge.

Catholic educators should investigate other curriculum options in their desire to get the most for their curriculum dollar. Since the Supreme Court has determined that Catholic schools cannot count on grants for teachers' salaries, schools may find themselves exploring some new approaches out of sheer necessity.

Instructional redesign is a possiblity where special tutors or learning consultants reduce the number of professional teachers required by a school. Some educators feel the professional staff could be reduced by up to 50 percent by adding such consultants. Schools may find themselves sharing faculty members—such as language consultants—as well as laboratories. Schools could also cooperate more on scheduling and curriculum planning. Brooklyn is trying many other methods of improving curriculum while controlling cost factors.

TECHNOLOGICAL CHANGES

In a controversial bestseller *The Greening of America*, Charles Reich refers to Consciousness III as ". . . a view of the world produced (as Marshall McLuhan first observed) both by the potential and the threat of technology."[35] Reich adds: "What we need is education that will enable us to make use of technology, control it and give it direction, cause it to serve values which we have chosen."

One of Reich's themes—man vs. machine—is summarized: "When man allows machines and the machine-state to master his consciousness, he imperils not only his inner being but also the world he inhabits and upon which he depends. He permits himself to be forced to exist in a universe that is, in the most profound sense, at war with human life."

Thus, Reich joins the forces of those who see that one of the crucial tasks confronting America is the proper use of technology. Nowhere is this more vital than in the educational process.

Yet, many of the promises made for technology in the sixties remained unfulfilled as the seventies began. Especially in the classroom, the impact of technology has been disappointing.

Technological changes require money. Consequently, many Catholic schools have struggled along without overhead projectors and science and language laboratories. Other Catholic schools (especially regional or diocesan schools) have been models in utilizing educational technology. It's possible to see both extremes in Catholic schools—the teacher who works with students in developing multi-media presentations, and the teacher who is afraid that showing a film is "entertainment" and certainly not worth spending class time on.

Are They Technicians or Teachers?

Any housewife who has had her oven go out of order just when company is expected for dinner can sympathize with a classroom teacher who is becoming more and more involved with the modern conveniences of education. Just as a mother's work is made lighter by her household gadgets, a teacher's lesson can be much more exciting when technical aids are used. Except when they don't work!

The machine has made everyone's life easier and the teacher is no exception. Some teachers drive to their schools in automobiles; they are only the first of many labor-saving devices upon which people depend.

In connection with the actual classroom lessons taught, a whole new technological industry has developed, one in which engineers are designing and producing items faster than teachers can learn how to operate them. There is a problem with many of these gadgets; the teacher is, figuratively speaking, caught in the middle concerning them. The teacher hears from administrators and educational officials that she should make use of slides and audio tapes in teaching. In addition, many of the students in her classes own cameras and portable tape recorders, equipment with which they are very much at home. The teacher may simply be frightened when faced with this pressure from both sides.

The real tragedy here is that learning tools exist that can help save the teacher's time. Isn't it ironic and sad that many teachers are too busy to employ time-saving educational tools?

Catholic schools have a special problem concerning technology however. This is the price tag the equipment usually carries.

Some time ago I read the following headline: "Teaching by Technology Can Save Catholic Schools." Here is the challenge thrown out to Catholics by Dr. Gabriel D. Ofiesh, Director, Center for Educational Technology, at the Catholic University of America in Washington D.C.: "Educational technology . . . is here to stay; its technologists are available and their tools are multiplying. Catholic schools could become the leaders of that revolution, making a quantum jump into truly quality education. If they refuse the challenge, the dire predictions about the end of Catholic education could come true."[36] If some responsible people actually believe technology can be a "savior" for Catholic schools, then educational leaders should explore this aspect of educational change closely.

Today's kitchen is very different from the one our great-great-grandmothers worked in. And very few people object to this. While "old-fashioned" cooking appeals to most people, an out-of-date kitchen doesn't.

Why shouldn't similar changes and improvements be reflected in our classrooms? Yet one teacher recently said to me: "If Horace Mann walked into most classrooms today, he wouldn't really see much going on that would astound him; he'd feel right at home." Horace Mann was an educational innovator (he lived from 1796 to 1859). As an educator, I feel

uneasy if it is true: in over one hundred years we haven't advanced beyond Horace Mann. We've had so much progress and innovation in all aspects of our lives, technology should help us improve our teaching too.

One of the ancient educational approaches (one that goes back far beyond Horace Mann) is simply described this way. A person who has some knowledge passes this information on to someone who doesn't have it. This passing-on-of-information can be accomplished many ways: by simply giving a speech about it; by having a discussion between the teacher and the student; by demonstrating what is to be taught, or by simply presenting the student with a problem and asking him to work out a solution on his own.

In ancient Greece, where schools or academies built a reputation we still try to follow, much learning was the result of discussion and debate over basic questions. We hear a great deal today about the need for dialogue. This was the educational technique Plato immortalized.

In the Middle Ages when great universities were first established, students traveled to these centers of learning and spent most of their time listening to lectures by great teachers. There were very few comforts available, but the goal of the student was to sit at the feet of the masters and absorb their ideas.

It is incredible that much of our educational approach today is still patterned after the medieval lecture method. Most of us who are teachers feel that we are really doing students a big favor if we share our knowledge with them.

It is true that what teachers have acquired should be transmitted to a new generation. This is the traditional passing on of a cultural heritage. But we are also faced with the problem of developing in students the basic equipment or tools for new learning. Today's young people will be grappling with questions and problems we haven't even heard of yet. This is why educational leaders—and Catholic leaders are among them—are trying to encourage teachers to make use of new materials.

What are some of these tools? Many different items are summarized by the broad phrase audio-visual, or media materials. This simply refers to items that can be seen or heard by the students. Such materials come in various sizes and shapes. Here's a sample of tools a teacher might use:

a photograph from *Life* magazine

a rock recording

a *National Geographic* "Special" on television

photographs of the lunar surface released by NASA

large maps and charts

an instructional television lesson received in the classroom

field trips out into the community

or an audio tape recording of the actor Richard Burton reading

love poems of John Donne, the 17th century metaphysical poet

Locating this material can be time-consuming, it's true. However, the above items can be much more effective in teaching than a monologue of a teacher which the students hear every day.

Some of these aids for teachers and students have been available for many years. Yet there has not been an enthusiastic response to them on the part of teachers. Why?

The teacher may feel that there is simply "too much to cover" in classes and she must simply keep talking as fast as she can to get it all covered so the students can be ready for the next grade-level. Of course, if Confucius was right and one picture is worth a thousand words, it may be that more visual presentations could teach concepts more effectively than the thousands of words students are subjected to.

The teacher may feel that she wants to teach the subject matter her way, without outside interference. Therefore, if learning materials, such as films, television programs, etc., are to be effective, they must be planned with the active cooperation of teachers themselves.

Another problem is that teachers may, when some TV programs are viewed, find them uninteresting.

Part of our problem when dealing with television is that many of us are used to receiving entertainment via TV in the evenings. We probably expect all television programs, even those designed for use in classrooms, to be entertaining for us. While education should be as enjoyable as possible, it is not sheer fun and, as we have said before, much of learning on a day-by-day basis is hard, disciplined work.

However, this is no excuse for poorly produced television programs. There are poor ETV programs, but I am certain that most educational television administrators are seriously trying to improve their quality. It is also true that there are many fine and exciting programs available, yet some teachers ignore them too.

These are just some of the reasons why some teachers still feel insecure with media. One solution to the problem is the proliferation of portable media equipment. Instead of receiving instructional television programs off the air, teachers may produce their own locally designed media materials. This guarantees that programs meet local needs and are available at convenient times for teachers and students. Each summer, the Boston Catholic Television Center, in cooperation with Boston College, conducts a Television Workshop to train teachers in preparing their own media materials. This six-credit graduate course has already trained many public and private school teachers in the use of media.

The Medium is the Massage

Most Americans were relatively unaware of the impact of media on their lives until someone mentioned that we are all massaged by media.[37]

Marshall McLuhan, the communications theorist, explained that media have such an impact on us we are almost all literally changed by it as it massages our minds. There is no doubt we are, as a society, almost totally different because of what technology offers us. What we want to explore here is how technology has affected education to date, and the technological opportunities available for Catholic education in particular.

For technology to be helpful to man, and especially to educators, it must be employed as a *tool*. It is an aid—designed to assist the teacher, the student, the parent, in learning and in life. Media, like other tools, can be helpful in the instructional situation if they are relevant to the learning involved, and if they are utilized properly. At a recent conference Mary Perkins Ryan urged caution. The audio-visual can be a gimmick, and we can become insensitive to its message.

What do we mean when we use the term media? The first thing that comes to mind would be television, simply because it is so obvious; it surrounds us. But media involve many other potential learning tools, such as film, slides, overhead projectors, audio tapes and cassettes.

Obviously these are significant learning tools. They can alter curriculum in schools and they are costly. Can Catholic education afford such alterations and such expense? The question really is: "Can Catholic education afford not to use them?"

One good thing about a crisis situation is that it almost forces one to try dramatically new approaches. Viewed as an impetus to experiment, Catholic educators cannot afford to ignore media. And they haven't ignored them.

One avenue for sharing media resources among Catholic educators is Instructional Television Associates—an organization uniting each diocese in America having its own closed-circuit diocesan television system.

There are nine American dioceses right now operating complete closed circuit television broadcast systems. All nine have joined Instructional Television Associates in order to coordinate plans, share programs, and purchase cooperatively. Those represented in ITA include the television systems of three New York areas (Yonkers, Brooklyn, and Rockville Centre), as well as San Francisco, Los Angeles, Detroit, Milwaukee, Miami, and Boston.

Since most of the dioceses represented are major urban areas, a large percentage of the Catholic-school children in America can be reached by these instructional television systems. This clearly indicates the communications potential for Catholic education. Most of the dioceses have three or four TV channels operating simultaneously to serve Catholic schools, Confraternity of Christian Doctrine Centers, and adult education programs.

Media Religious Education Project

One specific example of the potential for cooperative planning is a concept under development called the Religious Education Project (REP).

All dioceses represented in ITA, as well as other dioceses throughout the country, face the need for guidance in developing significant materials in the religious education area. Instead of having each group work out a program of study with local talent and resources, ITA members hope to coordinate planning, thereby making it possible to utilize national experts in theology, psychology and media production. Such curriculum materials could then be made available to Catholic educators on a national scale.

The project outline describes the overall objective: "To develop and implement a programmed course in Religious Education for elementary and secondary students which is modular in design, multi-media in approach, and validated unit by unit."

Some specific functions of the Religious Education Project are to: clarify the religious needs of students at different developmental levels; produce learning materials to match different learning styles of students; sequence behavioral objectives; identify qualified experts; identify production centers and coordinate production assignments; produce actual learning materials; validate materials used; develop a feedback system.

Learning materials could be developed and produced in various ways under the Religious Education Project umbrella. Units would probably be of varying lengths and grade levels. Thus, sequences could be planned around significant topics such as prayer, the personality of Christ, social action, ecology, etc. Some units might employ filmstrips, slides, film, and/or videotape. Materials could reach schools and CCD programs through the broadcast facilities of ITA members.

This type of imaginative (but very basic) curriculum development provides a rich blend of educational content and media enrichment.

The concept of the Religious Education Project closely resembles the approach of the Children's Television Workshop in developing *Sesame Street* learning units for broadcast. If this kind of organized, creative programming can be coordinated nationally by religious educators and media specialists, the Church will certainly be utilizing technology as a teaching tool.

Church leaders have been urged to make further use of media in the "Pastoral Instruction on the Means of Social Communication" issued by the Vatican in June, 1971. Noting that "the question is posed whether we are on the threshold of an utterly new sort of era in social communications ...," the document adds: "The modern media of social communication offer men of today a great round table. At this they are in search of, and able to participate in, a worldwide exchange of brotherhood and cooperation. It is not surprising that this should be so, for the media are at the disposal of all

and are channels for that very dialogue which they themselves stimulate. The torrent of information and opinion pouring through these channels makes every man a partner in the business of the human race. This interchange creates the proper conditions for that mutual and sympathetic understanding which leads to universal progress." And Pierre Babin, in *The Audio-Visual Man*, warns: "A Christian sees man's greatest liberation in Jesus Christ. Audio-visuals must not then be used simply as gimmicks to attract attention, but as a privileged language for proclaiming the 'Good News' of Jesus Christ for modern man."

Architectural Changes

Today's Catholic-school buildings are much like their public-school counterparts. Some are ancient and some remarkably modern. There are some differences when you place a Catholic school and a public school side by side. Very few Catholic schools have a gymnasium; many Catholic schools have had difficulties obtaining modern science labs. This type of costly physical plant may not be available to many Catholic schools simply because of the price tag.

Most Catholic-school buildings are in our vast urban centers. Many of these schools will be found in the central sections of major cities—even in the low-income areas where most of the immigrants who poured into this country resided.

You can imagine how difficult it is to attempt innovative and creative educational programs in a seventy-five-year-old building. And yet— for a century—many creative lessons have been underway in many of these classrooms. If we neglect to recognize this fact we do a disservice to a vast number of dedicated teachers. Many young students have discovered the excitement of learning in classrooms with old furniture. Perhaps the physical plant sets a tone for the educational search it houses, but education excitement *can* be generated within an old building.

Several other things about the physical structure of a Catholic school should be noted. There is usually a parish church or a chapel nearby. The non-lay teachers (usually part of a religious order within the Church) have lived in a nearby building constructed for them. (This has often made the faculty more available for school-connected activities after school hours. This fact may be altered as changes occur in the structure of religious communities.)

As we view the existing physical structure of a parish, we face several questions. Is it true that this physical plant is being used for only a small percentage of the people in the parish? How can we share these physical resources with more parishioners, youth and adult? Do we need to alter the physical plant somewhat in order to try new programs to meet the community needs? If a parish can no longer support a parish school, what should be done with the existing building?

The answers to the above questions are almost as varied as the locales of the buildings.

Leasing Schools

In some parishes the school may be leased to public-school authorities on a year-to-year basis, if it no longer functions as a parochial school meaningfully. This would mean that the administration and financing of the building during the school day would thus become the responsibility of public-school authorities. When the school day ends, the building is then available for parish activities—CCD classes, adult instruction, and other special parish functions.

The fact that the building is shared by two administrations could be difficult. It might be hard primarily because we're not used to it; however, just because we've never done a thing before is no reason to think it can't be tried now. Why can't we still accomplish things that are difficult? It was extraordinarily difficult building the Catholic-school system in the first place, but it was accomplished. We shouldn't lose our nerve in accomplishing additional difficult things.

School leasing contracts will probably have to undergo some legal testing also. Some educators have suggested that a type of religious counseling office or a religion resource area might remain available in a leased building, through which ecumenical groups could make information available to students. The Supreme Court has not ruled out teaching *about* religions in public schools and this type of resource library could expedite the study of the world's major religions. However, such a delicate area would have to be approached carefully so Catholics would not violate the constitutional guidelines in the process.

Leased schools could provide new opportunities for educational ecumenism—cooperation between public-school and Catholic-school administrators, teachers, and students.

As Church leaders plan to do some different things in these Catholic school buildings, it may be necessary to make architectural changes in them.

THE PHYSICAL PLANT IN CATHOLIC EDUCATION

If a building that was a parochial school is turned into a Religious Education Center, it may be necessary to tear down some walls to create rooms for showing films to large groups. You might have to turn some classrooms into smaller areas for group discussions. You probably ought to have some very small and private areas in the building for individualized guidance and religious counseling for people—both youth and adults.

However, before costly construction changes are undertaken, parish councils may find it worth their while to get guidance from the diocesan school board. Perhaps an education-architectural consultant can be hired by the diocese to provide advice and assistance to local church leaders facing such reconstruction work. This obviously, should not be a consultant who has a firm standing by to make the changes. This provides a strong temptation to encourage costly change. Whatever the diocese has to pay for this professional consultant will probably be repaid if only one school is able to save money by not making costly errors.

Other structural changes in our physical plants might include such things as air conditioning, so the buildings can be used effectively throughout the summer months. This idea might seem like a ridiculous suggestion to make to Catholic education authorities when there is a question of financial survival. However, the question is not just how much money you have; the question must be: What do you do with your money?

The problem is similar to the family budget problem of priorities. Why is it that one family seems to make their money go further than another family who might have the exact income and same number of children? It's probably because the first family has a plan—a systematic method of figuring out the ways to make the most efficient use of their limited income. This means going without some things, it means waiting a while for some things, but it might mean spending a lot of money on some things that in the long run will save you money.

Similarly, people supporting the parish are getting a lot more for their money if the funds are spent wisely to get the ultimate use out of their physical buildings.

These questions of costs are legitimate, for example, when people wonder whether technical apparatus like television equipment, overhead projectors, and film projectors are worthwhile. The question is not just the price tag, but what the parish is getting for its money.

Obviously, if the investment in such equipment purchases almost unlimited educational program resources, the parish may be getting more than in the purchase of something more limited in scope. The bill for the technical equipment might be less than the cost of the total labor and supplies for buildings and grounds. Media materials *should* come ahead of floor wax on our list of priorities. It should be obvious in such a case that the money spent on efficient learning tools brings more of a return to the parish. It's a better investment for parish funds and will bring back greater dividends. This is the type of budget analysis necessary when considering where to spend limited parish resources.

On a diocesan level, it may be possible to get more for the money. It has been estimated that a diocesan-wide television broadcast operation—which can serve the entire diocese in countless ways—can be built for the cost of building one school gymnasium. Thus, building a diocesan-wide communications system could be the most economical decision for a diocese, even though it will cost the diocese hundreds of thousands of dollars.

All physical alterations must be gauged by our concepts of experimentation and evaluation. A few schools that are converted physically into community centers, shared-time operations, or religious education centers should then be closely evaluated. In this way officials can see if the expected improvements have resulted, and what unexpected pitfalls have been encountered.

The next step—and it's a vital one—is to share the news. A small program could be developed, perhaps with slides and an audio tape, so it could easily be sent around to parishes and schools. Perhaps an Open House program could be set up on a regular basis, so people could come in and see what is being done elsewhere and evaluate this approach for their own location.

This is only one way to prevent what is often happening now in Catholic education (and, indeed, in education generally). Without coordination of efforts and sharing of ideas, you can develop the disease known as "duplication of effort."

What about new buildings? This matter is daring because most Catholic educational leaders are today saying that in many cases we have put up too many buildings already. And it is probably true that there should be a period of re-evaluation of our resources before expanding any further.

However, in some cases population shifts will force Church officials to face the problem of what kind of church and religious educational buildings will best serve the new parish areas.

The trend seems to be toward smaller chuches where a real sense of community can develop. Most buildings erected recently tend to more functional lines. America is a practical nation, which is probably one reason our philosophy of church architecture would never produce the majesty of the Gothic cathedrals of Europe. The current return to simplicity and community in religious worship will dictate building needs of the future.

NEW FORMS OF ALTERNATIVE SCHOOLS

Catholics have maintained separate schools for many years to provide a meaningful alternative to public schools. Convinced of the value of choice, parents have supported an entire system as a viable alternative.

The 70s are witnessing new forms of alternative schools, and Catholic educators and parents are beginning once again to reassess the value of diversity.

Called "new schools," "community schools," "free schools," or "alternative schools," these groups, although diverse, have similar characteristics. There must be free choice involved for the educational clientele—students and parents. Such a school must have a program that is significantly different from the conventional course of studies. Community involvement is essential in planning, development, operation and evaluation. There is a specific geographical location for the facility.

This new type of alternative school has gained momentum—growing from 46 in 1967 to 436 in 1970, an increase of approximately 800 percent.

The East Harlem Block Schools constitute a prime example. These schools are a fully parent-controlled, decentralized system of schools whose structure is unique in many ways. Any parent with a child in the school is automatically a member of the corporation. The East Harlem Block Schools have four programs: two nursery school/day-care centers for children from three to five, a year-round tutoring program, and a demonstration elementary school. There are 375 children in the programs, and 71 neighborhood people who work in the schools either full- or part-time. High-school equivalency and college-preparatory courses are available for those who are interested.

Many Catholic educators still feel that a full school program—offered as a meaningful alternative—is the most effective vehicle for integrating Christian values with all of learning and life.

What makes a school Catholic?

Robert L. Faricy, S.J., says the uniqueness of a Catholic school is that

1. In a Catholic school, religion is taught, and it is taught explicitly and as religion.
2. In a Catholic school, explicitly Christian witness is given by the teachers and there is explicit educational experience of the Christian community.

The school prepares persons to participate in God's creative activity by helping to build the world, and the school itself is a participation in that creative process. It is not only that the specifically Christian element of the curriculum adds to the humanistic elements of the curriculum a special Christian dimension. It is, rather, that the Christian and the human should not be separated.

Faricy predicts: "In the future we can expect many more religious education centers, bigger and better-staffed CCD programs, more trained and dedicated persons given entirely to the religious education of elementary school children, teen-agers and adults. We are moving into new and more complex situations, and they call for new and more diversified approaches."

Dr. George Elford notes that parents are experiencing new canonical, psychological, and cultural freedom to choose between a Catholic and a public school. Catholic people, therefore, must have presented to them a clear image of what the Catholic alternative school is.

Kraushaar concludes: ". . . It may be the special destiny of private schools to perfect counter-cyclical 'models' of the humanizing school dedicated to reawakening in the young the sense of community between old and young and the continuity of past, present, and future of the human adventure."

Many denominational schools (Catholic educators among them) would want to add to this humanizing process a special faith dimension, built upon appropriate religious beliefs and values.

And even the Catholic school system offers diversity. One unique choice is the Christian ecumenical school. This is projecting a new form within the existing alternative system.

Beyond School Reform

An educational study issued in 1972 was bound to evoke controversy, and, indeed, it did. Boldly asserting that schools have few long-term effects on the later 'success' of those who attend them, the study is entitled: *Inequality: A Reassessment of the Effect of Family and Schooling in America*. (Basic Books, 1972). The *Inequality* data involved 570,000 students in 4000 schools.

One author, and chief spokesman for the study, is Christopher Jencks, of Harvard, who also helped design the voucher proposal drawn up for the United States government. Jencks says that Americans have long turned to schools to solve problems; now, however, some people are beginning to look for new solutions.

In seeking more realistic alternatives to schooling over a four-year period of research, the *Inequality* authors reached three general conclusions:

1. Poverty is a condition of relative, rather than absolute, deprivation. People feel poor, and are poor, if they have a lot less money than their neighbors. This is true regardless of their absolute income.
2. The reforms of the 1960s were misdirected because they focused only on equalizing opportunity to "succeed" (or "fail"), rather than on reducing the economic and social distance between those who succeeded and those who failed.
3. Making schools more equal will not help very much. Differences between schools have very little effect on what happens to students after they graduate.

Jencks notes in the *Saturday Review of Education*: "The main policy implication of these findings is that although school reform is important for improving the lives of children, schools cannot contribute significantly to adult equality. If we want economic equality in our society, we will have to get it by changing our economic insitutions, not by changing the schools." (September 16, 1972).

In his discussion of poverty, Jencks redefines "the cost of living." It is "not the cost of buying some fixed set of goods and services. It is the cost of participating in a social system." He adds: "raising the incomes of the poor will not eliminate poverty if the cost of participating in 'mainstream' American life rises even faster." And his conclusion reinforces the title of the study: "eliminating poverty, at least as it is usually defined in America, depends on eliminating, or at least greatly reducing, inequality."

Jencks summarizes the basic assumptions underlying our past attempts to reduce poverty and he balances each with his own research results.

Past Assumptions	Jencks Research Data
1. Eliminating poverty is largely a matter of helping children born into poverty to rise out of it.	1. Poverty is not primarily hereditary. There is economic mobility from one generation to the next.
2. The primary reason poor children cannot escape from poverty is that they do not acquire basic cognitive skills.	2. There are many other equally important factors. IQ differences have as much effect on economic success as the effects of family background.
3. The best method of breaking this "vicious circle" is educational reform.	3. There is no evidence that school reform can substantially reduce the extent of cognitive inequality.

Jencks admits this research does not answer the question *why* school quality has so little effect on test scores. He suggests three possible explanations (and these concepts have appeared in Catholic school research also).

1. Children seem to be more influenced by what happens at home than by what happens in school.
2. Administrators have very little control over those aspects of school life that do affect children.
3. Even when the schools exert an unusual influence on children, the resulting changes are not likely to persist into adulthood.

The conclusion that "equalizing opportunity cannot take us very far toward eliminating inequality" must be evaluated by current advocates of school finance reform. This should be weighed by supporters of the court battle to eliminate dependence upon local property taxes for school finance. The Jencks research seems to warn that, even if all schools receive equal financial support, we will not eliminate inequality. Rather, his research seems to suggest that "adult success must depend on a lot of things besides family background, schooling, and the cognitive skills measured by standardized tests."

In a comment reflecting the philosophy of the voucher (as well as the hard-nosed realities of New York's Fleishmann Report), Jencks says: "There is no evidence that professional educators know appreciably more than parents about what is good for children."

Jencks adds some practical advice for educational reformers. He claims reformers are always claiming too much for what they propose. (He notes this applies to vouchers—his own reform—as much as any other innovation.)

What are the implications for social reform, Jencks asks in *Inequality*? "Until we change the political and moral premises on which most Americans now operate, poverty and inequality will persist at pretty much their present level." Jencks, therefore, calls for radical reform—going beyond schools, to social and political restructuring. He admits, realistically, however, that such reforms simply are not popular. Some commentators have noted an obvious drawback of the Jencks study: it is heavily committed to using personal income as the chief criterion for success. While many Americans may judge success in personal income terms, almost every American would know of a truly successful human being, whose salary might be lower than colleagues who, with higher paychecks, have not truly achieved success. There seems to be a gradual build-up of studies which should be analyzed by educators, and parents, when working through the current challenges of educational reform. In 1966, James S. Coleman, a sociologist at Johns Hopkins University, issued study results finding that non-school factors, such as family background, are more important in determining educational achievement than anything connected to the school. The Jencks study, which re-evaluates the Coleman Report, also builds upon a study by Dr. Daniel Moynihan. Moynihan's work seemed to reaffirm Coleman's finding. All three studies have provoked controversy concerning the research models and the results. These study results and procedures must be critically evaluated; they do not have to be accepted, but they cannot be ignored. Another controversial educational reformer has gone beyond schools—has actually called upon us to "deschool society." The term provides the title of a controversial book by Ivan Illich. It is a theme that John Holt and other educational reformers are embracing. In *Freedom and Beyond*, Holt claims that individuals are educated much more by the whole society around them and the general quality of life in it, than by what happens in our schools.

PART IV

Education
for
the
twenty-first
century

A popular song a few years ago spoke of dreaming an impossible dream, and this exercise in hope has always been the pastime of prophets.

In teaching, I have always enjoyed exploring the concepts of Utopia with students. Today, especially, youth are asking the question: "What is the perfect society? Students are interested in comparing the model offered by Thomas More in the sixteenth century with the modern scientific-consumer utopia of *Brave New World* or the structured society of Skinner. Oscar Wilde, the writer, said: "A map of the world that does not include Utopia is not worth glancing at for it leaves out the one country at which Humanity is always landing."

This book, too, could quite usefully conclude by asking the question: "What directions should be taken in education in order to achieve the impossible dream—the greatest possible educational growth for each human being?"

If we can accomplish other apparently impossible dreams, like walking on the moon, do we dare aim for anything less in our educational utopia?

Consideration of the thought of Teilhard de Chardin has encouraged many people to look toward an evolving future. Chardin likened education to the maturation of an individual human being. "Through education, mankind gradually acquires the knowledge of its birth, its history, its natural environment, its external powers and the secrets of its soul." The twenty-first century will offer its own challenges. It's not too early to begin getting ready for them. These challenges are not unique to Catholic education. They must be met by public and private educational agencies, working closely to achieve shared utopian goals.

The key challenge of education in any age is contained in the word opportunity. In the impossible dream, everyone—without exception—would have a chance to grow according to the individual's own potential. People will never be alike; however, their opportunities for growth should be the same. This means that in America's ghettos, as well as in undeveloped nations, people would have a truly equal opportunity for training. "Training" does not necessarily mean a college education. Vocational programs will be perpetually training and retraining people. Individuals will be prepared for jobs we haven't even conceived of yet. What the job description is really isn't important; what is important is that we make a real commitment to practical vocational training goals.

America, historically, has made a bold attempt at universal education. Such attempts may be made by other nations, also, but these educational programs can benefit from America's experience. What we have been able to accomplish must now be individualized and humanized. We have seen vast hordes rush through our educational systems, but often personal growth has been neglected because of sheer numbers.

This over-all challenge to humanize instruction should be unique as an aspect of all Catholic educational programs developed for the future. We will need tailor-made, individualized instruction programs to offset the effects of automation upon us and the depersonalized society in which we live.

Thus, education of the future must be available to everyone and must be more humane. This is a lot for any culture to achieve, but we should dream impossible dreams.

Individual growth requires educational support systems. This means that a single way is not necessarily the best way. The education of the future should probably resemble a supermarket, one in which each individual person is able, with assistance, to select the items that will be helpful. There might always be a few basic staple products everyone needs (ability to read, do simple computation, etc.). However, hopefully, many opportunities will be provided and people can select from them according to their own individual needs.

Such flexibility requires that on-going guidance is available. Often an individual is unable to visualize his aims or objectives clearly. The opportunity to discuss these goals with a counselor will help clarify an individual's needs.

Educators have already discovered that the structure we have built needs alteration. Several new directions show promise for our educational utopia.

For one thing, students are already beginning to move away from the school for educational experiences. In the open campus program, many students are leaving school to learn from outside agencies such as art museums, parks, libraries, courts, offices, forests, and even trips abroad. And, in this and many other programs, students are assuming more and more responsibility for their own learning.

It is not unlikely that in the twenty-first century much education will take place in a variety of locales, with a great deal of it occurring at home. Technology will make it possible to have many educational experiences without going to a specific school building.

The reformer Ivan Illich argues that schools will have to be de-emphasized (and society itself will have to be reconstructed) permitting people to be more fully human.[1]

Especially for adults, education must be accessible. According to Indian economist, Dr. J. C. Mathur, only .002 percent of public resources in the world are now available to adults. Because of the rate of change facing us, we must provide an on-going opportunity for individuals to up-date their knowledge long after any formal schooling has ceased. We have referred to this need in terms of vocational training. With increasing leisure time, adults must have educational opportunities available. Not everyone will want to use all his leisure in a learning situation; complexities of the twenty-first century will demand relaxation to provide a balance. But, like our educational supermarket, such opportunities when available, provide interesting choices for the people who need them, or simply desire them.

Hopefully, educators of the twenty-first century will make effective use of technology, more than we have so far. When properly utilized as learning tools, machinery can quite literally free education from the bonds of time and place. A computer, a television set, programmed materials, audio-visual cassettes—all these learning aids should be part of the stock on our supermarket shelves.

One unfortunate outgrowth of our commitment to universal education in America has been the degree of inflexible structure necessary to achieve this goal in the past. To handle large numbers we had to mass produce education. In an assembly line very little flexibility is permitted. This certainly must change in our educational utopia. Immediate practical examples would include flexible modular scheduling programs and elementary school individualized instruction programs.

One sunny afternoon recently I was visiting Sturbridge Village, in Massachusetts—a regional museum of rural American life. This peaceful retreat is a recreation of an imaginary representative New England community of the period 1790 to 1840, the first fifty years of the American Republic.

One leaves the busy highway behind and enters this two-hundred acre retreat with its village green, its white-spired New England church, its one-room schoolhouse, and other buildings, including a blacksmith shop, a gristmill, covered bridges, and herb gardens.

In this unique setting I reflected that America has moved quickly from the rural atmosphere reflected here to our modern-day society with its rigorous educational requirements.

Nostalgia from our past will not solve our present problems. But it does remind us that as America changes, her educational needs will also change.

America must be prepared for change. John Gardner warns: "The true task is to design a society (and institutions) capable of continuous change, renewal, and responsiveness."[2]

Thus, educational innovation must be provided in more creative ways in the future.

And Catholic educational programs must reflect creativity as well. This probably will involve more sharing of facilities: Church and community will cooperate in trying new joint ventures, such as community learning centers. These centers, with close cultural ties to their neighborhoods, could be combined high school and post high school, continuing education institutions. This should be a combined private and public responsibility for a decent environment. Qualified laymen will have a more responsible role to play in this ecumenical educational utopia.

If daring and courageous action is taken, a newly-designed Catholic educational system could serve as a meaningful alternative in America.

This demands courage—a special brand of courage. "It is the courage that reaffirms the divine spark of our humanity. And of our humanism."[3]

In an interesting contrast, two writers recently examined Catholic schools: one has looked to her Catholic past, and one has gazed into the hopeful future.

In the *New York Times* magazine (October 10, 1971), Caryl Rivers reflected upon her youth in a Catholic school. "I have walked since then in a wider world, one that pays scant attention to Our Lady of Fatima. But I remember growing up Catholic with affection . . . the smaller things are adhesive; they stick to the walls of my mind, anchoring the idea of God, making it impossible to root Him out."

Looking forward, instead of backward, Michael O'Neill shares his vision. "I look to a future in which tough, aggressive and imaginative Catholic educators will begin again to unfold the potentialities of the Christian school idea. I wait to witness the slow exhilaration and new strength which will come when the schools finally extricate themselves from the entangling alliances of the past. I look to a day when Catholic Christian schools will clearly be 'gospel communities of freedom and love.'"

The constant kaleidoscope

AN EPILOGUE

The Catholic educational scene today is extremely complex and varied—like the changing symmetrical patterns in a kaleidoscope.

A dramatic shift in the shape of Catholic schools occurred on June 25, 1973, when the United States Supreme Court ruled out several forms of aid to nonpublic schools, including the tax credit format.

In a series of 6-3 decisions, the Court ruled that the following laws "have the impermissible effect of advancing religion":

- • • a New York state law which provided "maintenance and repair" grants to private, nonprofit schools serving low-income areas;
- • • another section of the same law that provided tuition grants up to $100 for tuition-paying parents of nonpublic school children if the parents' annual income was below $5,000;
- • • a third section of the New York law which gave tuition-paying parents a deduction from gross taxable income in computing their state income tax;
- • • a Pennsylvania law that reimbursed parents up to $150 if they were paying tuition to send their children to nonpublic schools.

In the period preceding this decision, nonpublic school supporters had attempted to formulate legislation which would pass the three-part test *previously* suggested by the Court. The Court earlier mandated that a bill must have a secular intent; it must not have the *primary* effect of advancing the interests of religion or of religious institutions, and it must avoid "excessive entanglements."

As a result of a national drive to encourage support for federal tax credits, a bill was introduced in Washington to provide a tax break of up to $200 per nonpublic school child.

The Fordham law professor, Charles M. Whelan issued an analysis of the Supreme Court decision. Father Whelan noted that the Court "served clear notice that it will strike down any program that contains the potential for massive subsidies, direct or indirect, for education in (Catholic) schools." Whelan noted that the programs considered suffered from "three fatal defects": Catholic schools received most of the aid; the monies involved could be expanded to massive subsidies at a later date; and public schools and parents did not share the aid. Whelan concludes: "The odds are overwhelming that any new programs, whatever their form, that suffer from these same three flaws will not survive constitutional attack. . . ."

Several commentators have noted that the Court's reiteration of the "political divisiveness" doctrine is extremely dangerous to all churches and religious organizations. According to this argument, aid to education is unconstitutional because some churches are for it and some churches are against it. Whelan calls this "an incredible proposition, given the rest of the First Amendment (free speech, free press, free assembly, free petition of the government . . . .)"

With this shifting kaleidoscope, Whelan urges constancy of purpose: "We are going to have to make it at least for the time being, on our own and with the familiar forms of governmental assistance. Whether we have the will or resources to do that remains to be seen. I have no doubts that it is worth doing."

Repercussions in Catholic schools will follow these decisions. These will include some closings, increased tuitions, greater use of volunteers and paraprofessionals, and greater involvement of lay people in school policy. All these testify to the need for a basic realignment in educational policy. A recent editorial in a Catholic paper commented that if Catholic school problems are going to be solved they are going to be solved through a process open enough to involve those whose interests are at stake. If Catholic schools are going to be saved, it will be because enough Catholics want them.

While Catholic educators and parents began to assimilate the reality of the latest Supreme Court decision, the Watergate phenomenon rose as a component of America's modern cultural history. From the Watergate literature arises a theme appropriate for current Catholic educational reflection. Recognized by his family as an ambitious youth, one Watergate witness had been warned by an uncle: "Don't forget, John, to take the time to smell the flowers." The witness ruefully remarked: "Today I am taking the time to smell the flowers."[1]

Just as this individual was warned to slow down and reflectively assimilate things, Catholics now face a serious soul-searching process concerning the church's educational goals and the best way to meet these needs.

One such seriously reflective analysis was completed before the Supreme Court decision, but has become even more significant in the light of that decision. Rev. Michael J. Dempsey, Secretary for Education in the Brooklyn diocese, did his research at Fordham University. The in-depth study offers, I believe, challenging insights, along with a bold statement of daring directions for religious education in the Church's current educational crisis. An analysis is offered here in the hope that as Catholics understand these directions, they will reflectively build an awareness of objectives and processes into schools, and will, ultimately, lay the foundation for a reformulation of a Catholic philosophy of education.

The Dempsey study is an attempt "to analyze five key areas within which new directions for religious education have been indicated by the Second Vatican Council and developments in technology."[2] Five areas of research were isolated:

1. Faith as a dimension of life
2. How the Church (and the Christian) sees herself
3. Emphasis on Experiential Religious Learning and designing schools as a Christian Community
4. Emphasis on freedom and the individual
5. Technology

Information was gathered from official church documents, from twenty-one in-depth interviews with Catholic educators, and from questionnaires gathered from Catholic education personnel. Some of the conclusions reached:

- ● ● There have been extraordinary changes of direction for American Catholic schools as a result of Vatican II and technology, with very substantial practical implications for the schools.
- ● ● Relatively little work has been done in translating these changed directions into feasible instructional designs and programs.
- ● ● Some changes were a part of developing new theological insight, but for other changes there was little historical preparation.

163

● ● ● There is a failure to realize that technology and communications media are at the root of the culture change and thus at the root of new approaches to religious education.

These data call for a significant alteration of the design and management of schools as learning systems. While facing this need, the Catholic school system of the United States "does not possess an articulation of itself in terms of the new vision of the Council."

Changes of direction in religious education include: an understanding that Faith is a total commitment, not mere intellectual assent; an acceptance of the role of experience and the growth of community; an awareness that freedom is "a capacity to be cultivated"; an understanding of the need for close interpersonal relationships, etc.

In his new definition of schools, Dempsey calls for institutions to be an instrumentality in the faith process, "open to and altering its instructional design to meet the religious learning needs of the student. . . . The school is to be a laboratory, a point of interaction between the student and real life in a controlled environment. . . . It must be individualized to recognize and serve the unique."

Perhaps the educational challenge facing Catholics today can best be summed up in the words of the leading Catholic educational reformer Paulo Freire.

Freire, a Brazilian by birth, describes education as the practice of freedom in his book *Education for Critical Consciousness*.[3] The book opens with the sentence "To be human is to engage in relationships with others and with the world." Freire develops this concept by explaining that men "relate to their world in a critical way." In this evaluative/educational procedure, men respond to the challenge of their environment and "they begin to dynamize, to master, and to humanize reality."

Freire reflects:

And in the act of critical perception, man discovers his own temporality. Transcending a single dimension, he reaches back to yesterday, recognizes today, and comes upon tomorrow.

FOOTNOTES:
Introduction

1 "Has the Church Lost Its Soul?" *Newsweek*, October 4, 1971
2 "Can The Catholic Revolution Succeed?", *Redbook*, May, 1969
3 "The Catholic Crisis," *Commonweal*, January 7, 1972
4 Source of periodical figures: 1972 *Ayer Directory of Publications. Theological Studies*: 5,863; *America*: 62,970; *Catholic World*: 16,000
5 *The Official Catholic Directory*, 1972 (New York: P. J. Kenedy & Sons)

Part I

1 "Decline in Catholic Schools Ratified by Computer Data," *National Catholic Reporter*, November 27, 1970
2 Harold A. Buetow, *Of Singular Benefit: The Story of Catholic Education in the United States* (New York: Macmillan, 1970, p. 285
3 *The Official Catholic Directory* (New York: P. J. Kennedy & Sons, 1965)
4 National Education Association, *Estimates of School Statistics, 1970–1971* (Washington, D.C.: National Education Association, 1971)
5 Buetow, *Of Singular Benefit*, p. 285
6 Total decrease of Catholic school enrollments according to the *Official Catholic Directory* for the last five years.
7 Buetow, *Of Singular Benefit*, p. 167
8 *Ibid.*, p. 225
9 National School Public Relations Association, *Education, USA* (Washington, D.C.: National School Public Relations Association), p. 92
10 National Education Association, *Estimates of School Statistics, 1970-1971* is the source for public-school costs. Catholic-school costs released by the National Catholic Educational Association in *A Statistical Report on Catholic Elementary and Secondary Schools for the Years 1967-68 to 1969-70* (Washington, D.C.: NCEA, 1970), p. 19
11 Citizens for Educational Freedom, *Freedom in Education* (Washington, D.C.: CEF, Nov.-Dec., 1969), p. 5
12 "Support Growing for Parochial Aid," *New York Times* (June 16, 1969), p. 1
13 "N. Y. Board of Rabbis Shifts Stance on Aid," *The* [Boston] *Pilot* (January 30, 1971), p. 1
14 *Ibid.*, October 10, 1970, p. 29
15 Citizens for Educational Freedom, *Freedom in Education* (Washington, D.C.: CEF, March-April, 1970), p. 1
16 *Ibid.*, p. 1
17 *Ibid.*, p. 3
18 Letter to the author from E. P. Cullinan, Chief Deputy, Supreme Court of the United States, dated December 2, 1970.
19 The National Catholic Education Association uses a "contributed services formula" in connection with the salaries of religious. For example, a nun could receive $1800 as a basic fee and an additional $2000 room and board equivalent. (The parish provides the convent residence for the sisters.) The NCEA would estimate her salary as $2200 of contributed services.
20 NCEA "Data Bank" wage scale figures reported in *The* [Boston] *Pilot*, December 19, 1970
21 New England Catholic Education Center, *Educational Study, Archdiocese of Boston, Volume I, General Report* (Boston: Boston College, 1969), Recommendations No. 2 and No. 1
22 Timothy F. O'Leary, *The* [Boston] *Pilot*, August 17, 1968, p. 15

23 Edwin Wakin and Joseph Scheuer, "The American Nun: Poor, Chaste, and Restive," *Harper's* (August, 1965), p. 40
24 All staff statistics from *The Official Catholic Directory* (New York: P. J. Kenedy & Sons)
25 Benedictus, Saint, Abbot of Monte Cassino, *The Rule of St. Benedict* (London: Burns Oates, 1960). Edited and Translated by Abbot Justin McCann.
26 Felician A. Foy (ed.), *1970 Catholic Almanac* (Garden City: Doubleday & Co., Inc., 1970), p. 540
27 Kenneth Westhues, *The Religious Community and the Secular State* (Philadelphia: J. B. Lippincott Co., 1968), p. 62
28 Neil G. McCluskey, "The Education of Our Sisters," *America* (April 23, 1960), p. 119
29 Pope Paul VI, *Perfectae Caritatis*, October 28, 1965
30 Gabriel Moran and Maria Harris, *Experiences in Community* (New York: Herder and Herder, 1968), 205 pp.
31 Gabriel Moran, *The New Community* (New York: Herder and Herder, 1970), 134 pp.
32 Reported in *Education, USA* (December 21, 1970), p. 92
33 Andrew M. Greeley, *Symposium on The Future of the Church*, Boston, Massachusetts, April 11, 1970
34 Lawrence H. Fuchs, *John F. Kennedy and American Catholicism* (New York: Meredith Press, 1967), 271 pp.
35 Daniel Callahan, *The Generation of the Third Eye* (New York: Sheed and Ward, 1965), 249 pp.
36 Alvin Toffler, *Future Shock* (New York: Random House, 1970), 505 pp.
37 *Ibid.*, p. 141. This statement was made by Federal Communications Commissioner Hilliard
38 Gabriel Moran, *The New Community*, p. 33
39 Harvey Cox, *The Secular City* (New York: Macmillan, 1965, 1966), p. 15
40 Daniel Callahan (ed.), *The Secular City Debate* (New York: Macmillan, 1966), p. 118
41 Cox made this statement in a question-and-answer period during a Paulist lecture series in Boston, Massachusetts

Part II

1 Charles E. Silberman, *A Crisis in the Classroom* (New York: Random House, 1970), p. vii
2 Andrew M. Greeley and Peter H. Rossi, *The Education of Catholic Americans* (Chicago: Aldine, 1966), p. 270
3 Kenneth Clark, *Civilisation* (New York: Harper & Row, 1970), p. 347
4 James A. Burns, *The Growth and Development of the Catholic School System in the United States* (New York: Benziger Brothers, 1912), 421 pp.
James A. Burns, *Catholic Education—A Study of Conditions* (New York: Longmans, Green & Co., 1917), 205 pp.
J. A. Burns and Bernard J. Kohlbrenner, *A History of Catholic Education in the United States* (New York: Benziger Brothers, 1937), 295 pp.
Harold A. Buetow, *Of Singular Benefit* (New York: Macmillan, 1970), 526 pp.
5 Robert G. Hoyt (ed.), *Issues That Divide the Church* (New York: Macmillan, 1967), p. 78
6 George N. Shuster, *Catholic Education in a Changing World* (New York: Holt, Rinehart & Winston, 1967), p. 18
7 *Ibid.*, p. 65

8 Clark, *Civilisation*, p. 17
9 Walter M. Abbott (ed.) *The Documents of Vatican II* (New York: America Press, 1966), p. 675
10 Buetow, *Of Singular Benefit*, p. 26
11 John Gilmary Shea, *History of Georgetown College: Memorial of the First Centenary* (New York: P. F. Collier, 1891), p. 9
12 Kohlbrenner, *A History of Catholic Education in the United States*, p. 137
13 *Ibid.*, p. 48
14 *Ibid.*, p. 187
15 Thomas T. McAvoy, "Public Schools vs Catholic Schools and James McMaster," *The Review of Politics* (January, 1966), p. 19
16 William E. Brown and Andrew M. Greeley, *Can Catholic Schools Survive?* (New York: Sheed and Ward, 1970), p. xi
17 McAvoy, "Public Schools vs Catholic Schools and James McMaster," p. 19
18 *Ibid.*, p. 45
19 John Courtney Murray, *We Hold These Truths* (New York: Sheed and Ward, 1960), p. 39
20 Buetow, *Of Singular Benefit*, p. 220
21 John Tracy Ellis, "American Catholics and the Intellectual Life," *Thought* (Autumn, 1955), pp. 351-388
22 *Ibid.*, p. 386
23 *Ibid.*, p. 387
24 Mary Perkins Ryan, *Are Parochial Schools the Answer?* (New York: Holt, Rinehart & Winston, 1964), 176pp.
25 Silberman, *A Crisis in the Classroom*, p. 9
26 Theodore R. Sizer (ed.), *Religion in Public Education* (Boston: Houghton Mifflin Co., 1967), p. 112
27 John Courtney Murray, *We Hold These Truths*, 336 pp.
28 Silberman, *A Crisis in the Classroom*, p. 6
29 Sizer (ed.). *Religion in Public Education*, p. 232
30 Gerald C. Treacy (ed.), *Five Great Encyclicals* (New York: The Paulist Press, 1939), p. 65
31 Walter M. Abbott (ed.), *The Documents of Vatican II* (New York: America Press, 1966), p. 637
32 Joseph H. Fichter, *Parochial School: A Sociological Study* (Notre Dame, Indiana: University of Notre Dame Press, 1958), 495 pp. In this study Fichter notes: ". . . no thorough-going scientific examination of the parochial school has been made. . . ."
33 William E. Brown and Andrew M. Greeley, *Can Catholic Schools Survive?*, p. vii
34 Andrew M. Greeley and Peter H. Rossi, *The Education of Catholic Americans* (Chicago: Aldine, 1966), $8.95. The paperback edition is Doubleday Anchor No. 603 and costs $1.75.
35 George H. Gallup, Jr. and John O. Davies III, *Gallup Opinion Index: Special Report on Religion* (Princeton, 1969)
36 New England Catholic Education Center, *Educational Study: Archdiocese of Boston* (Boston: Boston College, 1969) Vol. I, No. 50
37 Greeley and Rossi, *The Education of Catholic Americans*, p. 231
38 William E. Brown and Andrew M. Greeley, *Can Catholic Schools Survive?* (New York: Sheed and Ward, 1970), 210 pp.
39 *Ibid.*, p. 3
40 *Ibid.*, p. 18
41 *Ibid.*, p. 22
42 *Ibid.*, p. 37
43 *Ibid.*, p. 41
44 *Ibid.*, p. 43

45 C. Albert Koob and Russel Shaw, *SOS For Catholic Schools* (New York: Holt, Rinehart & Winston, 1970), p. 130

46 Greeley and Rossi, *The Education of Catholic Americans*, p. 230

47 *Overview: A Continuing Survey of Catholic Trends and Opinions* (The Thomas More Association), April 15, 1970, p. 2

48 F. J. Sheed, *Is It The Same Church?* (Dayton, Ohio: Pflaum Press, 1968), p. 6

Part III

1 President Nixon's 1970 Education Reform Message to Congress, as reported in the National School Public Relations Association study, *Religion and the Schools*, 1970, p. 7

2 National Catholic Educational Association, *A Statistical Report on Catholic Elementary and Secondary Schools for the Years 1967-68 to 1969-70* (Washington, D.C. National Catholic Educational Association, 1970) p. 19

3 Russell Shaw, "Financing Cathoiic Education," *America* (September 28, 1968), p. 241

4 National Catholic Educational Association, *A Statistical Report*

5 "Majority Favors Keeping Schools Despite Expense," *The* [Boston] *Pilot*, July 4, 1970

6 "Survey Shows Faithful Would Retain Schools," *The* [Boston] *Pilot*, March 27, 1971, p. 10

7 *Catholic School Journal*, February, 1968

8 George Elford, "The Hidden Agenda," *America* (May 29, 1971), p. 560

9 "Gallup Poll Indicates School View Change," *The* [Boston] *Pilot* (February 16, 1963)

10 "Catholic Parents Unjustly Taxed, Says Billy Graham," *The* [Boston] *Pilot* (June 5, 1970)

11 Tracy Early, "The School Aid Question: Jews Take a New Look," *Catholic World* (June, 1970), p. 134

12 Sue Cribari, "Constitutional 'Bugs' Plague Nonpublic Aid," *The* [Boston] *Pilot*, (June 19, 1970), p. 10

13 *Ibid.*

14 "Hutchins Says Wall of Separation Has No Future If Taken Literally," *The* [Boston] *Pilot* (February 19, 1963)

15 Ralph E. Winter, "Crumbling Wall: Public Aid to Schools Operated by Churches Increases Despite Foes," *The Wall Street Journal* (Tuesday, November 10, 1970)

16 All Supreme Court Cases taken from official government records

17 William E. Brown and Andrew M. Greeley, *Can Catholic Schools Survive?* (New York: Sheed and Ward, 1970), 210 pp.

18 Michael O'Neill, "Plusses and Minuses in School 'Survival'", *Momentum* (February, 1970), p. 47

19 Center for the Study of Public Policy, *Education Vouchers: A Preliminary Report on Financing Education by Payments to Parents* (Cambridge, Massachusetts: Center for the Study of Public Policy, March, 1970)

20 Phillip Whitten, "Education Vouchers for the Poor," *Boston Sunday Globe Magazine* (February 14, 1971) p. 10

21 Neil G. McCluskey, *Catholic Education Faces Its Future* (New York: Doubleday and Company, Inc., 1968), p. 19

22 National Catholic Educational Association, *Voice of the Community—The Board Movement in Catholic Education* (Washington, D.C.: NCEA, 1967), 47 pp.

23 Daniel R. Davies and James R. Deneen, *New Patterns for Catholic Education—The Board Movement in Theory and Practice* (New London: Croft Educational Services, 1968), 133 pp.

24 National Catholic Educational Association, *Voice of the Community*, p. 12

25 New England Catholic Education Center, *Educational Study, Archdiocese of Boston* (Chestnut Hill: Boston College, August 1969)

26 William E. Brown and Andrew M. Greeley, *Can Catholic Schools Survive?*, p. 166

27 George A. Kelly, "A Department of Education and How It Grew," *NCEA Papers,* Series II, No. 1 (Washington, D.C.: NCEA), p. 4

28 *Ibid.,* p. 9

29 James J. Byrne, *Evaluate . . . Adapt . . . Innovate . . .* (Dubuque, Iowa: Board of Education and Educational Planning Commission), February 9, 1969

30 Joan M. Raymond, *The Evaluation of the Chicago Board of Education Experiment in Shared Time from September 1965 to June 1969* (Chicago: Board of Education, June 1969)

31 Letter to the author from Betty J. Bourgeois, of the Franklin County Northwest School District No. 7

32 National Education Association, Research Division, *Shared Time Programs: An Exploratory Study* (Washington, D.C.: NEA, April, 1964)

33 Robert C. Bealer and Fern K. Willits, "Religious Interests of High School Youth," *Insight* (Winter, 1968), pp. 35-36

34 "Catholic Educators Predict Changes," *National Catholic Reporter*, November 13, 1970, p. 9

35 Charles A. Reich, *The Greening of America*, (New York: Bantam Books, Inc., 1970)

36 Gabriel D. Ofiesh, "Teaching By Technology Can Save Catholic Schools," *The* [Boston] *Pilot*, August 23, 1969

37 Marshall McLuhan and Quentin Fiore, *The Medium is the Massage*, (New York: Bantam Books, Inc., 1967)

Part IV

1 Ivan Illich, *De-Schooling Society* (New York: Harper & Row), 116 pp.

2 John Gardner, Godkin Lecture, Harvard University

3 Abram L. Sachar, Brandeis University *Bulletin*, June, 1968

Epilogue

1 *Time*, July 9, 1973

2 Michael J. Dempsey, "An In-Depth Study of Five Key Changes of Direction Indicated for Catholic schools by Vatican II and Technology" (Fordham Doctoral Dissertation, 1973).

3 Paulo Freire, *Education for Critical Consciousness*, (New York: The Seabury Press, 1973)

IMPORTANT DATES
History
of
Catholic
Education
in
America

Early Establishment: European Culture is Transplanted to America
1494   First Mass celebrated in the New World
1565   First Catholic parish of the United States founded at St. Augustine,
                Florida
1642   First educational legislation passed in Massachusetts directing that
                children be taught to read "and to understand the principles of
                religion and the laws of the country"
1647   Massachusetts passes its law requiring towns to establish schools
1653   The first bequest in support of Catholic education in the colonies,
                Edward Cotton's will endows a Catholic school at Newtown, Mary-
                land
1727   Ursuline Sisters arrive from France to open first Catholic school in
                New Orleans
1747   The Jesuits establish a school for boys at Bohemia Manor, Cecil
                County, Maryland
1791   French Sulpicians open first seminary in the United States—St.
                Mary's in Baltimore: Georgetown Academy begins classes
1809   Mother Elizabeth Bayley Seton establishes the first native
                American sisterhood at Emmitsburg, Maryland

Transition: America Moves from an Agricultural to an Industrial Nation
1829   American bishops hold the First Provincial Council of Baltimore
1839   First public normal school (teacher-training school) established in
                Lexington, Massachusetts
1844-45   Orestes A. Brownson and Isaac T. Hecker received into the Catholic
                Church
1852   The First Plenary Council of Baltimore
                Massachusetts passes first compulsory school attendance law
1856   Sigmund Freud is born
1857   Opening of American College at Louvain (Belgium)
1858   Founding of the Paulist Fathers—the first native religious com-
                munity for men in the United States
1859   Publication of Origin of Species by Charles Robert Darwin
                John Dewey, the American philosopher is born
                The North American College opens in Rome
1862   Land-grant colleges are established (Morrill Act)
1866   The Second Plenary Council of Baltimore
1869   Charles Eliot elected President of Harvard—elective system is un-
                veiled
1875   "Instruction to the Bishops of the United States Concerning the
                Public Schools" is issued, dealing with the danger to religious faith
                of children in public schools, and the need for parish schools
1884   The Third Plenary Council of Baltimore
                A strict command is issued: Pastors must build parish schools and
                parents must send their children to them. Pope Leo XIII later writes
                to Cardinal Gibbons endorsing a separate Catholic school system for
                America

Growth: Naturalism, Pragmatism and Darwin

1887	Gibbons in Rome (to be made Cardinal) praises Church-State relations in the United States
1888	First Superintendent of Schools is appointed in New York (Rev. William J. Degnan)
1889	Opening of the Catholic University of America
1890	Archbishop Ireland delivers address on public and private schools before the National Education Association in St. Paul
1891	Rev. Thomas Bouquillon issues a pamphlet entitled *Education: To Whom Does It Belong?* Booklet enunciated the idea that education belongs to the parent, the church, and the state.
1893	First Catholic college for women opened—College of Notre Dame of Maryland, in Baltimore
1900	*The Interpretation of Dreams*, by Sigmund Freud, is published
1904	Founding of the National Catholic Educational Association
1918	National Education Association issues "Cardinal Principles of Secondary Education" listing American public school educational goals
1925	The Scopes trial highlights the contest between the fundamentalist viewpoint (William Jennings Bryan) and the new science (Clarence Darrow)
	Supreme Court decision Pierce v. Society of Sisters—the Oregon state law requiring all children to attend public schools was unconstitutional
	Publication of *Experience and Nature*, by progressive educator John Dewey
1927	Publication of *Human Nature and Conduct* and *The Public and its Problems*, both by John Dewey

Maturation and Modern Times: Communism, Sputnik, and Soul-Searching

1929	Pope Pius XI issues the encyclical on "The Christian Education of Youth"
1930	Supreme Court decision Cochran v. Board of Education upholding a Louisiana statute providing textbooks at public expense for children attending public or parochial schools
1947	Supreme Court decision Everson v. Board of Education of the Township of Ewing, that a school district in New Jersey did not violate the United States Constitution by paying transportation costs for Catholic school pupils
1948	Supreme Court decision McCollum v. Board of Education, declaring unconstitutional a program for releasing children, with parental consent, from public school classes so they could receive religious instruction on the public school premises
1952	Sister Formation is established as an organized attempt to improve the background and educational training of nuns in American Catholic schools
	Supreme Court decision Zorach v. Clausen, that it was constitutional to release students from public school classes, on a voluntary basis, for religious instruction given off public school premises
1957	Sputnik is launched by Russia and a massive re-evaluation of America's educational system begins
	John Tracy Ellis challenges the intellectual maturity of America's Catholics
1963-64	Peak of enrollment in America's Catholic school system

1964	Publication of *Are Parochial Schools the Answer?* in which Mary Perkins Ryan seriously questions whether an organized school system is part of the essential mission of the American Catholic Church
1965	*Declaration on Christian Education* is issued by the Vatican Council and Pope Paul VI
	Declaration on Religious Freedom is issued by the Vatican Council and Pope Paul VI
1966	Harvard University issues a study of Religion in Public Schools
	The National Opinion Research Center issues the Greeley-Rossi report on *The Education of Catholic Americans*
	The Carnegie Corporation of New York issues the Notre Dame Study of Catholic Elementary and Secondary Schools in the United States: *Catholic Schools in Action*
1968	Supreme Court decision Board of Education v. Allen, declaring constitutional the New York school book loan law which requires local school boards to purchase books with state funds and lend them to parochial and private school students
1970	Supreme Court decision Walz v. Tax Commission affirming tax-exemption for houses of religious worship in America
1971	Supreme Court decisions Lemon, DiCenso, and Tilton, stating that federal aid to sectarian colleges is permissible under the Constitution, but that "purchase of secular services" at elementary and secondary level constitutes "excessive entanglement" of church and state in America
1973	Supreme Court struck down New York and Pennsylvania laws which would have provided partial reimbursements to parents who paid tuition to non-public schools

HISTORICAL STATEMENTS CONCERNING SCHOOLS FOR CATHOLICS IN AMERICA. . . .

". . . we judge it absolutely necessary that schools should be established in which the young may be taught the principles of faith and morality, while being instructed in letters."

> First Provincial Council of Baltimore 1829

"The education of the rising generation is . . . a subject of the first importance; . . . we have . . . sought to create colleges and schools in which your children, whether male or female, might have the best opportunities . . . you are aware that the success and permanence of such institutions rest almost exclusively with you."

> Pastoral of 1833

"There are few subjects dearer to us than the proper education of your children, on this mainly depends their true respectability in this world . . ."

> Pastoral of 1840

". . . in view of the very grave evils which usually result from the defective education of youth, we beseech (you) to see that schools be established in connection with all churches . . ."

> First Plenary Council 1852

"All are agreed that there is nothing so needful . . . as the establishment of Catholic schools in every place—and schools no whit inferior to the public ones." . . . Parents who neglect to give this necessary Christian training and instruction to their children, or who permit them to go to school in which the ruin of their souls is inevitable . . . if obstinate, cannot be absolved."

> Instruction to the Bishops of the United States Concerning the Public Schools 1875

". . . we decide and decree that near each church, where it does not exist, a parish school is to be erected within two years from the promulgation of this Council, and is to be maintained in perpetuum . . ."

> Third Plenary Council of Baltimore 1884

"Every Catholic . . . every man who loves truth and wishes to conform to it, must be in favor of Catholic schools and Catholic education, if they are Catholic in reality as well as in name."

Orestes A. Brownson

"The necessity for parish schools is hypothetical—the necessity being not a direct result of the church's mission, but a provision in certain cases for the protection of the faith. The church is not established to teach writing and ciphering, but to teach morals and faith, and she teaches writing and ciphering only when otherwise morals and faith could not be taught . . ."

Archbishop John Ireland in a letter to Cardinal Gibbons, December, 1890

". . . it is the inalienable right as well as the indispensable duty of the church, to watch over the entire education of her children, in all institutions, public or private, not merely in regard to the religious instruction there given, but in regard to every other branch of learning and every regulation in so far as religion and morality are concerned."

". . . the so-called 'neutral' school from which religion is excluded, is contrary to the fundamental principles of education. Such a school moreover cannot exist in practice; it is bound to become irreligious."

Encyclical Christian Education of Youth
Pope Pius XI
December 31, 1929

"Among all educational instruments the school has a special importance. It is designed not only to develop with special care the intellectual faculties but also to form the ability to judge rightly, to hand on the cultural legacy of previous generations, to foster a sense of values, to prepare for professional life."

"The influence of the church in the field of education is shown in a special manner by the Catholic school . . . Since, therefore, the Catholic school can be such an aid to the fulfillment of the mission of the people of God and to the fostering of the dialogue between the church and mankind, to the benefit of both, it retains even in our present circumstances the utmost importance."

"... the Catholic school is to take on different forms in keeping with local circumstances. Thus, the church considers very dear to her heart those Catholic schools, found especially in the areas of the new churches, which are attended also by students who are not Catholics."

Second Vatican Council's
Declaration on Christian
Education October 28, 1965

"... I am increasingly favorable toward Catholic schools . . . In a pluralistic society, it seems to me particularly useful to have schools which prepare people in significantly different ways than the public schools . . ."

Daniel Callahan, Spectrum of
Catholic Attitudes 1969